HOW TO IDENTIFY MUSHROOMS TO GENUS III

HOW TO IDENTIFY MUSHROOMS TO GENUS III: Microscopic Features

BY DAVID LARGENT
DAVID JOHNSON
ROY WATLING (Consultant)

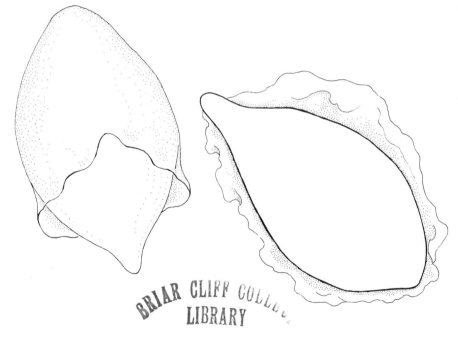

Illustrations: **KATHRYN SIMPSON**

David L. Largent
Department of Biology
Humboldt State University
Arcata, California 95521

David Johnson
Department of Biology
Humboldt State University
Arcata, California 95521

Roy Watling
Royal Botanic Gardens
Inverleith Row
Edinburgh EH3 LR5
Scotland

MAD RIVER PRESS INC.

© David L. Largent

Published by: Mad River Press Inc.
Rt. 2 Box 151 B
Eureka, CA. 95501

Printed by: Eureka Printing Co. Inc.
106 T Street
Eureka, CA. 95501

ISBN. 0-916-422-09-7

3624312-3

i

TABLE OF CONTENTS

List of Figures..iii
List of Plates..iv
I.   Introduction 1
II. Laboratory Techniques 3
     A. Checklist 3
     B. Equipment & Materials 4
     C. Calibration of a Microscope 7
     D. Techniques for Securing Hand Sections............8
     E. Planes of Sectioning: Radial, Tangential, Transverse
         (Cross)..11
     F. Dissection and Orientation......................14
     G. Rehydration of Dried Material...................18
     H. Techniques with Tube (& Teeth) Fungi............18
     I. Permanent or Semi-Permanent Slides 20
III. Chemical Reagents...................................21
     A. Wetting Agents 21
     B. Useful Companion Agents 22
IV. Hyphae 28
     A. Hyphal Systems 28
     B. The Hyphal Wall 30
     C. Septations......................................32
     D. Hyphal Branching 32
     E. Hyphal Inflations 35
     F. Specialized Hyphae.............................35
     G. Pigmentation 36
     H. Chemical Reactions 38
V.   The Pellis or Cortex
     A. Topography 44
VI. Trama
     A. Hymenophoral Trama (Context)...................60
     B. Pileus and Stipe Trama........................66
     C. Pigmentation 67
     D. Chemical Reactions 67
VII. Cystidia (Cystidium = Singular) 71
     A. Position 72
     B. Type of Cystidia (Morphology, Function, Origin) 72
     C. Shapes of Cystidia............................74
     D. Pigmentation and Incrustation 80
     E. Chemical Reactions 80
     F. References......................................81
VIII. Basidium and Basidiole
     A. Basidia..89
     B. Basidioles.....................................91
     C. Chemical Reactions 91

IX. Basidiospores
   A. How to Study Basidiospores 94
   B. Spore Features 95
   B. 1. Spore Color 95
      2. Spore Attachment 96
      3. Spore Symmetry 100
      4. Spore Size 101
      5. Spore Ornamentation 103
      6. Spore Shape 108
   C. Chemical Reaction of Spores 114
Literature Cited 120
Glossary, Index and Examples of Features 122

LIST OF FIGURES

Figure 1. Calibration of a Microscope 8
Figure 2. Sectioning Techniques 9
Figure 3. Planes of Sectioning 12
Figure 4. The Planes and Views of the Stipe 13
Figure 5. Blocks of Tissue................................15
Figure 6. Sectioning Techniques I 16
Figure 7. Sectioning Techniques II 19
Figure 8. Hyphal System................................29
Figure 9. Incrusted Hyphae..............................31
Figure 10. Inflated or Disarticulating Hyphae 33
Figure 11. Clamps and Cystidioid Hyphae...................34
Figure 12. Types of Pellis I...............................45
Figure 13. Types of Suprapellis (Pileipellis) I 46
Figure 14. Types of Suprapellis 48
Figure 15. Types of Suprapellis (Pileipellis) II 49
Figure 16. Types of Pellis II..............................51
Figure 17. Types of Pellis III............................ 52
Figure 18. Veils..54
Figure 19. Arrangement of Hymenophoral Trama 62
Figure 20. Subhymenium and Arrangement of Hymenophoral
        Trama..63
Figure 21. Gelatinized Gill Trama 65
Figure 22. Position of Cystidia.............................73
Figure 23. Types and Shapes of Cystidia 75
Figure 24. Cystidia Shape I 77
Figure 25. Cystidia Shape II..............................79
Figure 26. Spore Attachment 97
Figure 27. Parts of a Spore...............................98
Figure 28. Spore Attachment and Symmetry 99
Figure 29. Spore Wall 102
Figure 30. Spore Ornamentation I..........................104
Figure 31. Spore Ornamentation II 106
Figure 32. Spore Ornamentation III 107
Figure 33. Spore Shape I.................................110
Figure 34. Spore Shape II................................112
Figure 35. Spore Shape III 113
Figure 36. Spore Shape IV 115

LIST OF PLATES

I. Incrusted Hyphae ...39
II. Hyphae I ...40
III. Hyphae II ...41
IV. Clamps ...42
V. Pileipellis: Derm 1 ...55
VI. Pileipellis: Derm 2 ...56
VII. Pileipellis ...57
VIII. Pileocystidia and Pileipellis ...58
IX. Pileipellis ...59
X. Hymenophoral Trama 1 ...68
XI. Hymenophoral Trama 2 ...69
XII. Hymenophoral Trama 3 ...70
XIII. Cystidia: Position ...82
XIV. Lamprocystidia ...83
XV. Cystidia 1 ...84
XVI. Cystidia 2 ...85
XVII. Cystidia 3 ...86
XVIII. Cheilocystidia and Lamprocystidia Shape ...87
XIX. Cystidia 4 ...88
XX. Inaequihymeniiferous Hymenium and Holobasidia 92
XXI. Hymenium and Basidia ...93
XXII. Basidiospores 1 ...116
XXIII. Basidiospores 2 ...117
XXIV. Basidiospores 3 ...118
XXV. Basidiospores 4 ...119

PREFACE

In the modern or contemporary classification of agarics, and to some extent the boleti, microscopic features are emphasized, for the most part, over macroscopic features. Therefore, in order to understand the modern taxonomy of agarics and boleti, a thorough knowledge of microscopic features is an absolute requirement. To accomplish this, numerous literature sources need to be acquired, including several books and many published articles. Some of the articles as well as the books are "out-of-print" and therefore unavailable; others are available but are either difficult to obtain or if obtainable quite expensive.

For sometime now, we have felt that an inexpensive book is required in which microscopic features are tersely discussed and profusely illustrated; it is our desire that this book achieves these objectives. It is written with the intent to provide the student of fleshy fungi with a source of information with which a thorough study of mushrooms can be achieved and with which species and genera of agarics and boleti can be identified. The terms we have stressed, the features we have discussed, the illustrations we have used, and the method of presentation we have chosen, all have been accomplished with one idea in mind: to assist the student of agaricology in understanding the microscopic features used in describing and identifying agarics and boleti.

This particular book is written in such a way that it is a companion to another volume, keys to the families and genera of agarics using microscopic features. These two books should provide adequate information on the microscopic features of fleshy fungi. In combination with the first two volumes, *How To Identify Mushrooms to Genus: Macroscopic Features* and its companion volume on genera, the student of fleshy fungi should have a command of the field so that any additional study can be attempted.

Two individuals need to be commended for their work, Kathy Simpson, our artist, whose drawings are superb, and Pamela Largent, our typist, whose steadfastness assured us that not only would the book get done but it would be done correctly. Without them our endeavors would be meaningless.

Finally we wish you "good mushrooming".

David Johnson
David Largent
Roy Watling

Arcata, CA.
September, 1977

I. INTRODUCTION

In order to understand the microscopic features of agarics and boleti, a review of the terminology of the macroscopic features of the basidiocarp is necessary. The basidiocarp is divided into a pileus (or cap), a stipe (or stalk) and a hymenophore which in the case of agarics are the lamellae (gills) and in the case of boleti are tubes or pores. Remnants of either or both of two veils, the universal veil and the partial veil, can be present although both are frequently absent. The remnants of the universal veil can form patches (patch) or warts on the surface of the pileus and the volva (cup) around the bottom of the stipe. The partial veil can remain as a ring of tissue around the stipe, the annulus (ring), and/or as a piece of tissue on the margin of the pileus, an appendiculate pileal margin.

If a longitudinal section of a basidiocarp is made, the following regions or areas can be determined:

1) the veil remnants if any;

2) the surface of the pileus, the pileipellis (pileus cuticle) which is that outer layer of hyphae of the pileus morphologically distinct from the pileus trama;

3) the surface of the stipe, the stipitipellis (stipe cuticle) which is that outer layer of hyphae of the stipe morphologically distinct from the stipe trama;

4) the pileus trama (or context) which is that layer of hyphae between the pileipellis and subhymenium or the lamella (gill) trama; the pileus trama can often be distinguished from the hymenophoral trama by differences in color or

structure but if not by an imaginary line which separates the hymenophore from the pileus. It is that tissue which makes up the bulk of the pileus.

5) the stipe trama (or context) which is that layer of hyphae occupying the center of the stipe excluding the stipitipellis. The stipe trama can sometimes be distinguished from the pileus trama by changes in color or structure but if not it is demarcated by an imaginary line which separates the pileus from the stipe;

6) the hymenophoral trama (gill, lamella or tube trama), the layer of hyphae occupying the center of the hymenophore and microscopically distinct from the subhymenium or the pileus trama;

7) the subhymenium, a layer of hyphae immediately beneath the hymenium and morphologically distinct from the trama of the pileus or the stipe;

8) the hymenium, a layer of cells consisting of basidia, basidioles, and, if present, cystidia.

A tangential section of the pileus will reveal similar regions but from a different perspective.

A study of the microscopic features of a basidiocarp involves an examination of the hyphae and the elements (or cells) of the hyphae of which these regions are composed. Such a study not only involves the morphology of the cells and hyphae as seen through the lens system of a compound microscope but also the reaction of the hyphae to various chemicals.

This book is arranged in order to facilitate the study of the microscopic features of the basidiocarp. The first part of the book involves a discussion of the techniques which are used in the study. The second a discussion of the chemicals used in the study of the microscopic features and the third a discussion of the features of the structures of which all regions of the basidiocarp are composed. The fourth is a discussion of the morphology of the surfaces of the basidiocarp and is followed by a fifth portion that involves the context or trama of the pileus, the stipe, and the hymenophore. The next part is a discussion of the terminal cells of which the surfaces of the basidiocarp are composed, namely the dermato-, endo-, and hymenophoral cystidia. The seventh part of the book discusses the basidia and is followed by a separate discussion of the numerous basidiospores. The final chapter is a glossary and index, including a list of common species which can be used to demonstrate the features in this book.

Once the microscopic features have been studied and understood, it is our hope that the study of fleshy fungi will be continued. We strongly urge descriptions to be made of as many fungi as possible and a correlation of microscopic features with macroscopic features be attempted. *Remember!* Every macroscopic feature used to describe a basidiocarp has a set of microscopic features which can be correlated with it; for example, the pileus surface of a viscid to glutinous species of *Cortinarius* is represented by a particular kind of pileipellis called an ixotrichodermium; or the dark brownish color of certain *Naucoria* species is because of a pigment which incrusts the hyphal wall; or the marginate gill-edge of *Leptonia serrulata* is the macroscopic expression of the cheilocystidia being filled with a vacuolar pigment. When such correlations are made and understood, the student interested in the study of the fleshy fungi will have acquired the basic, fundamental knowledge prerequisite to all other studies in this fascinating field.

II. LABORATORY TECHNIQUES

Prior to studying the microscopic features of agarics and boleti, a set of materials should be accumulated and stored in a permanent container. For example, one of us (D.L.) uses a metal bait and tackle box which fishermen use to house their bait, tackle, flies and what not. This container has lots of compartments for the instruments needed to study the fungi. Most bait and tackle boxes are not heavy and have handles which facilitate carrying the container from one locality to another.

The following checklist of equipment and materials should be placed on a card and glued to the underside of the lid of the container.

A. CHECKLIST

Razor Blades
Sharpening Stone
Oil (for sharpening blade)
Microscope Slides
Cover Slips
Forceps (Tweezers)
Camel's Hair Brush
Probes (Dissecting Needles)
Lens Paper
Absorbent Material
Spot Plates

Dropper Bottle with
   Xylene
   Tap Water
   95% Ethanol
   3% KOH (5-10% NH$_4$OH)
   Teepol
Chemical Reagents
Eyepiece
Stage Micrometer
Note Paper or Cards
Pencil or Pen

4

B. EQUIPMENT AND MATERIALS

Razor Blades. We recommend three types of blade: 1) A single edged razor blades; 2) A double edged razor blade of the type used in a wide variety of razors. If you use this kind of blade you have to be careful about cutting your fingers. Recently we saw a student in a beginning Botany class eliminate this problem by taping one side of a double-edged blade with masking, medical or scotch tape; electricians tape would work as well. Double edged blades tend to be flimsy and bend which can result in irregular hand sections; this particular problem does not exist with a good single edged razor blade. 3) A barber's razor which can be sharpened with a strap or a stone; these were in use at the turn of the century. Such a blade is difficult to acquire nowadays; however, it has some advantages. It can be sharpened over and over again; it is sufficiently large to facilitate easy, smooth handling; and it is durable.

Since razor blades must be very sharp to obtain useable sections, it is best to obtain a supply of cheap, dispensible ones. If you use the single-edged or double-edged blades, plan to use quite a few and be prepared to throw them away as soon as you suspect the blades to be the slightest bit dull. One blade might last 5 or 50 sections; it all depends on the toughness of the specimens, the condition of the material (whether dried or fresh), and the edge of the blade (chemical reagents quickly oxidize the edge). Furthermore, it is desirable to have several blades in use simultaneously so as not to mix different sections or contaminate them with other chemical reagents.

Sharpening Stone and Oil. If you choose to use the barbers razor, a stone to sharpen the blade is necessary as well as a lubricant; the latter depends on the kind of stone used. A small thong of leather is essential to clear the cutting edge prior to each sectioning session.

Microscope Slides and Cover Slips. Indispensible in the study of microscopic features are the glass slides on which the sections will be placed. Slides used in a typical high school or biology class are acceptable; use slides which are fairly thin as the thick ones will impair the light when viewing through a microscope.

Cover slips vary in thickness which is usually indicated by a number; #'s 0-1 are very thin, #'s 1-2 moderately thin, and # 3's or above considered quite thick. If you want to observe spores or thin sections of the basidiocarp at the highest magnification possible (i.e. oil immersion with the highest power lens 100X), you should use those cover slips numbered 0-1. #2 cover slips will function satisfactorily when using objective lenses (4X, 10X, 43X).

Forceps (Tweezers) and a Camel Hair Brush. A pair of good forceps simplifies handling the thin, often wispy bits of tissue which will blow away with even a sigh of relief at having succeeded in cutting a good, thin section. We find the best forceps to be those with very fine tips, such as watchmaker's forceps (or #3's made by Inox). However, one can manage with the type of forceps found in manicure sets. A cork or rubber bung into which the tips of the forceps can be pushed protects the tips and prevents one being pricked.

A fine, camel hair brush is admirable for manipulating floating bits of tissue.

Probes or Dissecting Needles. These are instruments with a long needle-like end and either a wooden or metal handle. You need at least two to manipulate your sections, to tease apart bits and pieces of tissue and to remove debris from the sections. Excellent probes can be made by replacing the conventional metal probe included in student kits with an ordinary sewing needle pushed into a wooden handle made of a match stick.

One of us (D.L.) suggests a third probe in which the needle has been flattened; the flattened end of this instrument allows one to transfer sections without the aid of forceps. Furthermore, discarded dental instruments offer a range of shapes and probe tips which can be very useful to the mycologist.

Lens Paper. A soft, non-abrasive tissue paper should be used to clean off debris and liquid which inadvertently find their way onto the lenses of the microscope. Such tissue is commonly called lens paper and can be obtained from the same place as the immersion oil. It can be stored in a jar.

Absorbent Material. Some type of absorbent material is an absolute necessity and will be used to absorb excess liquids or to diffuse chemical reagents throughout a section. Paper towels function admirably, as will kleenex tissues. The latter can be purchased in small packets which would fit into a bait and tackle box.

Spot Plates. Although not an absolute necessity, chemical spot plates are convenient. Sections can be rehydrated or stained in various liquids Spot plates are particularly handy for working with dried material. They are constructed of porcelain or glass, vary in thickness from about 5-15 mm (with 5-10 being the most functional), and have from 3 to 12 depressions of about 1-3 mm in depth. We find it convenient to have 3 or 4 of these spot plates available. If you purchase porcelain ones, color and color changes of the sections can be easily noted.

Dropper Bottles. Various kinds of dropper bottles are available which are modifications of the old dropper bottles which contained nasal drops Dropper bottles are constructed out of plastic or glass and have a dropper which can function in or out of the bottle We suggest plastic dropper bottles in which the dropper is secured within a screw-top lid. These unbreakable, leak-proof bottles will house the chemical reagents used in the study of the microscopic features of agarics and boletes.

Immersion Oil and Oil Container. A good oil in which the 100X objective lens will be immersed can be obtained from any company which handles optical equipment. Such oil should be stored in a bottle which does not leak. Make sure your oil is of good quality as some brands have been shown to be carcinogenic.

Xylene. This universal solvent is a colorless liquid used to clean grime and immersion oil from objective lenses.

Chemical Reagents. A myriad of chemicals are used in the study of the microscopic features of agarics; some of which are used routinely and others more sporadically. Several liquids indispensible in the study of fleshy fungi should be included in the laboratory equipment. These are tap water, 95% ethanol, 3% Potassium Hydroxide (KOH) or 5-10% Ammonium Hydroxide (NH₄OH), and a wetting agent such as Teepol or a good liquid detergent, used to decrease the number of air bubbles prevalent in sections.

Formulae and uses for a wide range of chemical reagents can be found in Chapter 2.

Eyepiece (graticule) and a Stage Micrometer. Measurements of microscopic structures described in this book should be made in the standard unit of measurement, the micron (μm), which equals 1/1000 of a millimeter (mm). Measurements are accomplished with the aid of a calibrated eyepiece graticule or micrometer which consists of a piece of glass on which equidistant measuring units are etched. This piece of glass fits into one eyepiece of your microscope. The equidistant units need to be calibrated (mathematically made equivalent) into microns. Calibration is done with the aid of a stage micrometer; directions for this procedure are outlined on page 7.

Note Paper or Cards When studying the microscopic features of agarics or any other fungus, notes should be made on some sort of paper or file cards. One of us prefers to keep his notes on 8 x 11 paper on which all of the descriptive features have been printed; in this way a complete list eliminates the problem of forgetting one or two features, plus the features are listed in the same place on each paper which facilitates comparisons between collections and between taxa.

Pencil or Pen. Nothing is more infuriating than to begin work and not have any writing instruments available. Mechanical pencils are useful since lead replacements can be stored in the bait box. Wooden pencils are less expensive; however, keep an ample supply plus a sharpener in the box.

Hand Lens or Dissecting Microscope. A good hand lens which magnifies from 10-20X is essential for observing small features of both fresh and dried material. Binocular viewers which slip over the head are equally functional because they leave your hands free.

Educational institutions use dissecting microscopes which look like a pair of high power binoculars. The system uses two kinds of lenses: the oculars (the one you look through) and objectives. Ocular lenses usually magnify the subject 7.5-15X whereas objective lenses magnify the subject from .7-15X. By complementing each other the lenses magnify the subject from between 5 to 225 times normal size with most dissecting microscopes operating from between 7 and 30X total magnification. The best advantage of a dissecting scope is that it allows the material to be viewed over a large area.

Compound Microscope. A good student's microscope is all that is required to see the structures discussed in this book. The microscope should be equipped with both ocular and objective lenses.

Obviously one can spend a fortune on purchasing a microscope. What is necessary is to assure that the microscope has a total magnification power of between 30 and 300X; this can be accomplished by having ocular lenses of at least 7.5X and objective lenses of 4.5 (low power) and 40X (high power). Two other objective lenses are useful: 10X (moderate- or middle-power) and 100X (oil). Some systems incorporate a larger nosepiece for very low power (1.5X) which replaces the dissecting scope.

Adding a phase-contrast system to a compound microscope increases its effectiveness but it is not a necessity. Such a system often permits minute ornamentation of spores and of hyphae to be more clearly observed.

C. CALIBRATION OF A MICROSCOPE

Two pieces of equipment are required in order to calibrate a compound microscope, a stage micrometer and an ocular micrometer (also eyepiece, graticule, reticule).

A stage micrometer (Fig. 1A) is a thick glass slide in the middle of which is a scale mounted beneath a cover slip. The scale preferably is metric divided up into small and large units. A large unit is broken into a group of ten small units On one corner of the slide are two measurements, usually 1 mm and .01 mm, the larger indicating the distance between each of the large units and the smaller indicating the distance between each of the small units.

The ocular micrometer (Fig. 1B) is a small, round piece of glass which fits into an ocular lens tube and rests just above the lens. The ocular micrometer is also divided into small and large units. However, no measurements are indicated on it as these have to be calibrated for the focal length of a particular microscope.

Calibrating the eyepiece unit measurements needs to be done for each objective lens of the compound microscope. Most compound microscopes have three objectives – 25X, 10X, 40X; therefore, three separate calibrations will need to be done. Each objective will be calibrated in the same way.

Technique: Assume the 40X objective lens is in place. a) Place the stage micrometer so the scale is focused in the field of view of the microscope. b) Move the stage micrometer so that one line of the stage micrometer precisely coincides with one line on the ocular micrometer in the left side of the field of view. c) Moving to the right, find the next line of the stage micrometer which precisely coincides with a line of the reticule. Count the number of spaces of the stage micrometer between the lines which coincide at the left and at the right. (Suppose there are four spaces of the stage micrometer which correspond to 10 lines of the ocular micrometer, see Fig. 1C.) d) Divide the spaces of the stage micrometer by the spaces of the ocular micrometer (4 divided by 10). e) The result will be the number of stage micrometer spaces per ocular micrometer spaces (.25). f) Since each space of the stage micrometer equals .01 mm, (as written on the slide), each space of the ocular micrometer will therefore equal .0025 (.25 X .01) g) The appropriate unit of scientific measurement is a micron which equals 1/1000 mm and is abbreviated with the following symbol, μm. Convert the measurement of each ocular micrometer (.0025 mm) to microns by

8

moving the decimal point three spaces to the right; therefore each small unit of the ocular micrometer equals 2.5 μm. *Remember*: The calibration will change for each objective (lens) so the procedures need to be performed on each one. Furthermore, if the ocular lenses are changed in any way, new calibrations need to be made. For quick reference, write the results for each objective on a small card and tape it to the base of the microscope.

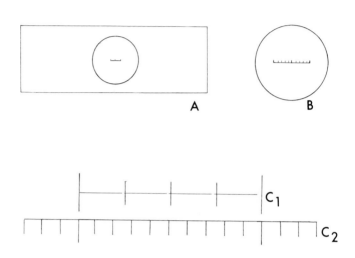

A   B

C_1

C_2

FIG. 1. **Calibration of a Microscope. A.** Stage Micrometer; **B.** Ocular Micrometer; **C.** Four lines of Stage Micrometer **(C-1)** corresponding to ten lines of Ocular Micrometer **(C-2)**.

D. TECHNIQUES FOR SECURING HAND SECTIONS

A number of ideas exist which will aid in securing the material. Three of these are as follows:

Probably the easiest, but the most dangerous, way to hold the material is by hand. Hold the material to be sectioned between the thumb and forefinger of one hand; the thumb is usually higher than the forefinger and the forefinger is usually at right angles to the thumb. (Fig. 2A) The raor blade is placed face down on the forefinger with the edge parallel to the tissue to be sectioned; thus the plane of the face of the blade is parallel to the desired plane of tissue. The blade is passed through the tissue with the thumb functioning as a backstop. Believe it or not, thin sections can be made in this manner, it just takes practice (and courage!). Obviously a sharp razor could easily cut a finger but with care and patience a cut thumb can easily be avoided. Put a piece of tape over the thumb when first doing this in order to judge the required pressure.

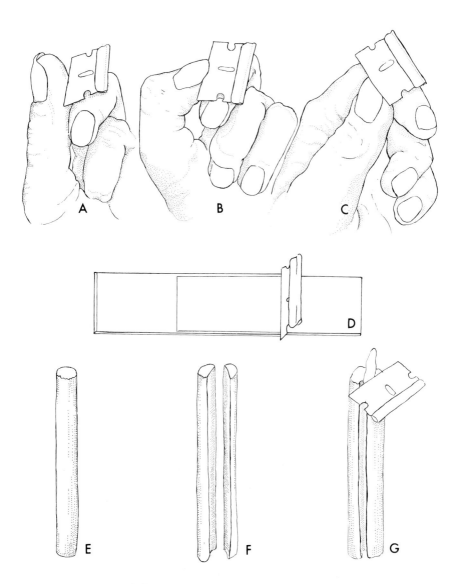

FIG. 2. Sectioning Techniques. A-C. The three ways to hold the razor blade using hand sections; D. The glass slide-sandwich technique; E. A piece of pith; F. Sectioning the pith in half; G. Situating the material between the halves of elderberry and the razor blade on the end of the pith.

Unbelieveable as it may seem, we have been using this technique for 15 years without cutting a thumb. Two variations are possible — one is to hold the thumb so just the nail protrudes above the forefinger (Fig. 2B) (long nails are a must); the other is to hold the thumb equal to or below the forefinger in such a way that the razor blade passes above the thumb (Fig. 2C).

The next technique is used by people who study algae or mosses and liverworts. Two glass slides are used — the material is placed in the middle of one slide while a second slide is placed over the material so that the sides of both line up. What results is a sandwich. The slides are the bread and the tissue is the baloney. Situate the material so that the place to be sectioned is parallel to the plane of the end of the slides. (Fig. 2D) Place the top slide so that one end exposes the material to be sectioned; expose only that amount of material you want as a section. Now pass the razor blade over the material using the end of the top slide as a guide and the bottom slide as a back. As the section is completed, move the top slide back the desired width of the section and pass the razor blade over the material again. Repeat the process over and over again. It is preferable to place both slides face down on the table and section downward.

A third way is to place the material between two pieces of elderberry pith (*carrots or potatoes can be substituted for elderberry pith*); Pith is a soft tissue composed of thin walled cells which will section easily. Take a piece of pith and cut it longitudinally into two halves (Fig. 2E-F). Make a sandwich with the material to be sectioned placed between the two halves of pith. Orient the material so that the plane of the desired section is parallel to the plane of the end of the pith sticks. Now firmly squeeze the pith sticks together and rest the razor on the end of the pith stick and pass the razor blade the desired thickness through the pith and therefore through the material (Fig. 2G). By passing the razor through the pith quickly and often, several sections will be produced and with practice, thin sections can be regularly accomplished.

Some hints: 1) Make a rather thick section the first time you pass the blade through the pith; this way the material between the pith will have a neat, complete cut from which good, thin sections can be made. 2) Wet the raor blade with a drop of water near the edge. This insures two things — it more or less oils the surface of the blade thereby cutting down the drag which could tear the material. Also the liquid provides a medium in which the sections will accumulate. 3) Make short, quick, firm and complete cuts with the razor. Do not stop in the middle of a section or use a herky-jerky motion as it will tear the material. 4) Always make sure your raor is clean and sharp.

The best sections are those you almost can't see with the eye on the razor blade edge. After many sections have been made, they usually accumulate on the razor, or the glass slide, or in amongst the pieces of pith. Make it a practice to scrape material from the razor into a drop of liquid using the long side of your probe or camel hair brush. It is convenient to float the material including bits of pith by means of a droplet of water. The sections will float easily from the razor onto a slide or into a depression plate. Before you mount your sections, check them under the dissecting scope or with a hand lens. Pick out the best sections with brush, forceps or the flattened probe and transfer them into a drop of liquid on a slide.

E. PLANES OF SECTIONING: RADIAL, TANGENTIAL, TRANSVERSE (CROSS)

Sections can be obtained from fresh material or from fungi which have been dried and stored in a herbarium. Hints on how to make such sections have been published by one of us (R.W.) and some of the following techniques have been adapted from his publications.

Agaricologists regularly use several kinds of sections when viewing microscopic detail. It is important to thoroughly understand the basic orientations of these sections to the basidiocarp and the features which each section will demonstrate. Once this is mastered, interpretations and observations of features will be much easier. Remember, practice makes perfect and the extra time taken in making thin sections will enhance the possibility of correctly interpreting sections.

An excellent suggestion is to purchase about one-half pound of mushrooms (*Agaricus hortensis*) from a local store, and practice with them in the following manner. Start by taking an entire basidiocarp; cut the stipe off at a point near AB as indicated in Figure 3. Set the stipe aside and place the cap on a piece of paper with the gills facing the paper (a spore print is made in a similar manner). Cut this cap on a line extending from one margin of the cap to the other margin, through the center. One such cut is labeled CDE (Fig. 3) and the resultant side view is diagrammed in Figure 3X. Any section equivalent to a radius of a circle (C-D and D-E are two such radii) constitutes a **Radial Section**. Now take another basidiocarp and again cut the stipe off at a point near AB. Again set the stipe aside and place the cap on a piece of paper with the gills facing the paper. However, cut this cap from one margin to the other but *not* through the center. One such cut is labeled FG (Fig. 3) and the resultant side view is diagrammed in Figure 3Y. Any section parallel to this plane is called a **Tangential Section** of the cap since it parallels the line FG which represents a tangent of a circle. Now take a third basidiocarp and again cut it at a point near AB. However, turn the cap this time so that the margin rests on a piece of paper. Cut this cap along the line indicated by HI (Fig. 3) and the resultant view is diagrammed in Figure 3Z. All sections parallel to this place are called **Transverse** or **Cross Sections** of the cap; note that the plane of this section is basically perpendicular to that of the radial and tangential sections both of which are kinds of longitudinal sections.

Pick up the three stipes of the three basidiocarps that have been set aside (Fig. 4). All of them are identical in appearance. Take one, cut it along a line outlined by JK; note that this line passes through the center of the stipe. The resultant plane of view of such a cut is diagrammed in Figure 4O. This exact plane is a specific type of longitudinal section (median) called a **Radial Section** of the stipe. Repeat the process on the second stipe but cut it along the line LM; note this cut does not pass through the center of the stipe. The resultant plane of view of such a cut is diagrammed in Figure 4P. This exact plane of view is a specific type of longitudinal section (non-median) called a **Tangential Section** of the stipe. Again repeat the process with the third stipe; however, this time cut the stipe as indicated in N. The plane revealed represents a cross sectional view and any section parallel to this view is called a **Cross Section** of the stipe (Fig. 4Q).

12

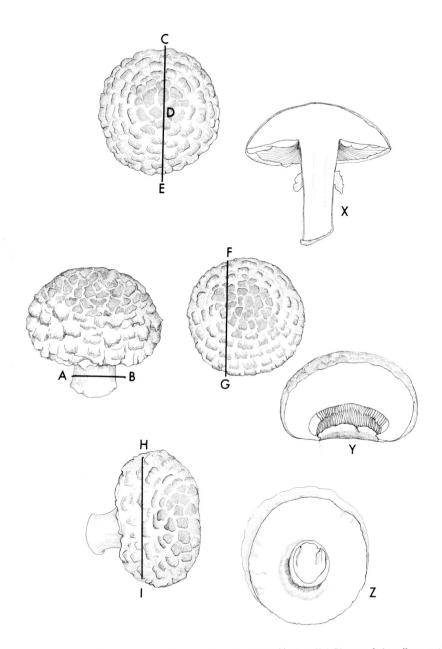

FIG. 3. **Planes of Sectioning** using *Agaricus hortensis*. **X.** A radial Planes of the pileus cut along line CDE; **Y.** A Tangential Plane of the pileus cut along line FG; **Z.** A Transverse Plane of a pileus cut along line HI; AB represents the line to cut when removing the stipe from the pileus.

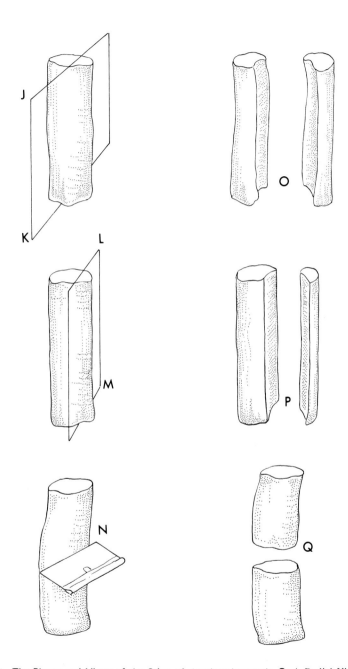

FIG. 4. **The Planes and Views of the Stipe** of *Agaricus hortensis*. **O.** A Radial View of the stipe cut along plane JK; **P.** A Tangential View of the stipe cut along plane LM; **Q.** A Transverse View of the stipe cut where indicated at N.

If numerous basidiocarps are available for study, sacrifice one for a spore print. When the basidiocarps are collected, cut the cap off of one near AB again and place the cap with the gills on a piece of paper or a glass slide. Wrap the entire cap, including the paper or slide, in waxed paper or cover it with a glass jar.

More often than not only one basidiocarp will be available for sectioning. Therefore become familiar with the diagrams of the single basidiocarp in order to maximize the observations utilizing the sectioning techniques.

Cut a single mushroom longitudinally in half, just as was done for the study of sections for *Agaricus*. Put one-half of the basidiocarp on a glass slide in a chamber containing damp paper or moss; the humidity created in the chamber will allow the cells of the tissue to retain their turgidity because they will often collapse if left in a dry atmosphere. Additionally a spore print may be made on the glass slide which will enable the spores to be studied microscopically. Make it a practice to put any part of a fruiting body which is not being examined into a similar container. Place the other half of the basidiocarp with the cut portion on some surface and view it under the dissecting microscope, under the lowest power of a compound microscope or with a hand lens. A cursory examination will provide excellent views of the pileus and stipe surfaces.

F. DISSECTION AND ORIENTATION

In practice, mycologists use only a portion of the pileus or stipe from which to cut hand sections, particularly in the case of the larger, fleshy fungi. Figure 5 shows several places to begin the dissection of the basidiocarp. Remember the plane of section (radial, tangential, or transverse) is still important. To obtain a good radial section of the pileus cut rectangular blocks of tissue along a radius (see Fig. 5, A,B,C). A slice along the long edge of these blocks is a tangential section of the pileus. A slice along the shorter edge would be a cross section of the pileus. Another convenient way to obtain tangential sections is to cut out a wedge shaped piece of the pileus (Fig. 6A,B). Fold the wedge to form a horseshoe shape in which the gill faces all touch one another (Fig. 6C). A slice at either end of this wedge yields a tangential section of the pileus. The advantage of removing only a part of the gill is to avoid very thick or oblique sections. Since a gill is wider nearest the pileus, it is best to trim off only the portion needed for study. The same is true for the stipe. By cutting out a small block of tissue, hand sectioning is made easier.

The following discussions provide techniques for studying the microscopic features of the Pileus, Lamellae, and Stipe.

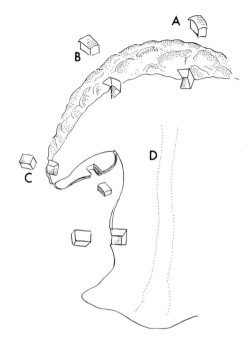

FIG. 5. **Blocks of Tissue** taken from the Pileus of *Agaricus hortensis*. **A.** On the Disc; **B.** Midway to the Margin; **C.** At the Margin. Block of tissue taken from the pileus flesh; **D.** In blocks B,C,D, sections parallel to the long side are Tangential and those parallel to the short side are Radial.

Pileus (Cap). Cut the basidiocarp along line AB (Fig. 3) and place the stipe into your moist chamber. Perform the following operations:

Make a thin radial section from the margin to the apex of the pileus so as to include one entire gill. Place this section in a drop of water on a glass slide into which Teepol or a liquid detergent has been added. Add a cover slip and observe under the low power of the compound or dissecting microscope. Observation of the section should provide you with the following: 1) the general configuration of the outer surface of the pileus, the **Pileipellis** (often called the "cuticle"); 2) the presence of absence of, as well as the relative abundance, shape and color of the sterile cells on the gill edge, the **Cheilocystidia**; 3) the composition of the central flesh of the pileus called the **Context** or **Pileus Trama**.

Make thin radial sections of the pileus surface **(Pileipellis)** so as to include as much of the pileus trama as possible. If possible, try to make the radial section on the pileus disc (apex) (Fig. 5A), midway to the margin (Fig. 5B), and at the pileus margin (Fig. 5C).

16

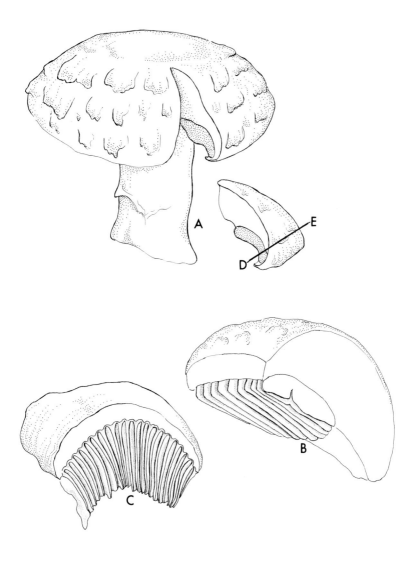

FIG. 6. **Sectioning Techniques I.:** *Agaricus hortensis.* **A.** A wedge taken from the pileus; **B.** An enlarged view of the wedge with the pileus margin cut off along the lines DE; **C.** The view of the gills being pressed together into a "horseshoe."

Place some sections in a drop of water on a glass slide into which Teepol or a liquid detergent has been added. Additionally place some sections into drops of selected chemicals and stains on a completely different slide. Observations of such sections should provide you with the following:

1) The shape of the **Pileocystidia**;
2) The location of the **Pigment** in the cells;
3) The type of **Pileipellis**:
4) The presence or absence of **Clamp Connections**;
5) The nature of the **Pileus Trama.**

Lamellae (or Gills). Remove a wedge of tissue from the pileus (Fig. 6A, B) so that several gills are included. Cut off the margin along a line DE and discard. Make the following sections from this piece of tissue.

Cut a thick tangential section through the pileus including several gills (in essence the tangential section shows the gills in cross section). Mount this section on a dry slide and observe under a dissecting scope, low power of the compound microscope or a hand lens. Then add water and Teepol and after adding the cover slip, observe again. Observations of such a section should provide you with the following:

1) The type of **Gill Trama** or **Hymenophoral Trama** (tube trama);
2) The presence or absence of as well as the realtive abundance of, sterile cells on the gill edge called **Pleurocystidia**;
3) The type of **Subhymenium**;
4) The number of **Spores** per basidium;
5) The type of pileus surface but in a different view (tangential compared to radial).

Cut thin tangential sections of the pileus so that they include several gills and gill edges. In addition to the features seen at low power the following structures can be observed: details of the basidia, of the hymenophoral trama, of the pileus trama, and of the pileus surface (the pileipellis).

Pileus Trama (or Context). Remove a small block of tissue from the pileus (Fig. 5D). Make thin sections of the end as well as the sides of the block of tissue. These sections will reveal the disposition of the pileus trama both in radial view (section the long side) and in tangential view (section the short side).

Stipe (or Stem). From the humid container, retrieve the stipe. Make radial, tangential, transverse (cross) sections as shown in Figure 4. Observe the nature of the stipe cortex often termed the "rind" or **Stipitipellis**, the **Stipe Trama**, the presence or absence of **Caulocystidia** as well as their shape, size and pigmentation.

Basal Tomentum. Finally, examine the basal portion of the stipe under the dissecting microscope or with a hand lens in order to determine if there are any remains of a veil and/or vegetative mycelium. If found, mount the material in water as well as in various reagents on separate slides.

Scalps. Thin slices from the surface of the pileus and the stipe are called "scalps" (fig. 7A,B,C). One scalp section should be taken from the pileus, and two from the stipe (one at the top and one at the bottom). Each section should be placed into a drop of water on a glass slide into which Teepol or a liquid detergent has been added. After placing a coverslip over the tissue, it is tapped gently to spearate the elements. Such sections will show if the pileus is composed of cellular (Fig. 7D) or filamentous units (Fig. 7E). Scalps of the stipe will not only demonstrate the cellular or filamentous units but also the presence, absence, shape and size of the caulocystidia. Furthermore, clamp connections can be easily demonstrated in all sections.

Care must be taken not to reverse the scalps either when transferring them to the liquid on the slide or by allowing the surface tension of the liquid to pull the section upside down.

G. REHYDRATION OF DRIED MATERIAL

The same procedures as outlined above for fresh material can be performed on dried material. However, it is necessary to revive and wet the material, thereby making it sufficiently pliable for sectioning.

Separate the pileus from the stipe of a dried basidiocarp just below the attachment of the gills. Place the entire pileus (if the basidiocarp is small) or a wedge-shaped piece of pileus (if the basidiocarp is large) into enough 95% ethanol in the well of a depression plate to wet the entire tissue. Leave the pileus in the alcohol for at least 30 seconds, after which the material should be transferred into tap water in another depression. Leave the material in the tap water until it becomes completely pliable. Blot the pileus with some absorbent paper, place the material between two pieces of pith and complete the same number and types of sections and of cuts as you did for fresh material.

Cut the stipe of the dried material into two pieces and then each piece longitudinally into two halves. Place these pieces into 95% ethanol and then water following the same porcedure as for the pileus.

H. TECHNIQUES WITH TUBE (& TEETH) FUNGI

Except for the study of the tubes, the techniques for studying the microscopic features of boletes are identical to those used in studying agarics. The tubes of boletes are often long and extremely fleshy. Unless one uses a sharp razor, sections can end up a sloppy mess. One of us (R.W.) prefers to section the tubes of dried basidiocarps rather than fresh, even to the extent of cutting a wedge of bolete material and drying it under an ordinary light bulb. He does not place tubes in pith or revive the tissue with liquids. Rather, sections of the tubes are made from intact, dried fruiting bodies which are subsequently revived in water or dilute alkali solutions.

Realize that the first sections of the tubes of many boletes contain an abundance of cystidia which will obscure the other constituents of the tubes. These sections should be rejected or kept separate from sections higher up the

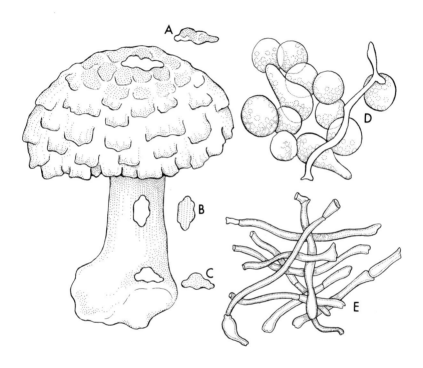

FIG. 7. **Sectioning Techniques. II.:** *Agaricus hortensis;* Scalps taken from the pileus **A.** or from two places **B.,C.** on the stipe. **D.**Cellular units of the pileus of *Bolbitius;* **E.**Filamentous units of pileus of *Galerina.*

tubes. It is often very useful to cut the tubes in half in order to avoid confusion between cheilo- and pleurocystidia.

Once a number of cross sections have been obtained, place these in a few drops of 95% ethanol or water in the depression of a spot plate for 10 to 15 seconds; then transfer the sections to tap water in another depression.

Longitudinal sections of the tubes should again be taken from dried material and preferably with some of the pileus flesh attached. They should be treated in the same manner as the cross sections. Longitudinal sections will show:

1) type of tube trama (hymenophoral trama);

2) the presence or absence of, as well as the relative abundance of pleurocystidia;

3) the type of lateral stratum and subhymenium;

4) the number of spores per basidium;

5) the shape and characters of the cheilocystidia which form a flange to the tube orifice.

Radial sections emphasize the characters and structure of the tube trama.

I. PERMANENT OR SEMI-PERMANENT SLIDES

All sections can be made permanent. To make permanent slides, influx Hoyer's medium or balsam and ring the cover slip with fingernail polish. Unfortunately this often results in causing the sections to become abnormal through plasmolysis or unusual swelling.

Semi-permanent slides can be made by completely ringing the cover slip with a mixture of 1 part beeswax, 2 parts lanolin or vaseoline and 4 parts paraffin. Such a mixture has a low melting point but solidifies quickly after melting. It spreads easily and is impervious to air and liquids. Be sure to keep the mixture intact all the way around the cover slip and to store the slides face up. One of us (D.L.) has kept such slides for over one year in good condition.

Sections can also be mounted in gum chloral and kept for long periods without deformation. Other proprietory polymerizing resins and polyvinyl alcohols designed for microscopy are also useful.

III. CHEMICAL REAGENTS

Many of the chemical reagents are corrosive and/or toxic. Care should be taken not to get the chemicals on any part of the microscope, on any clothing or on any part of the body. If chemicals are spilled, they should be cleaned up immediately; clothes and any part of the body should be thoroughly flushed with water.

All chemicals should be used on clean slides and unless otherwise indicated used one at a time on a slide. This is particularly important with Melzers, for example, which forms a precipitate when mixed with an alkali, like potassium hydroxide (KOH) and ammonium hydroxide (NH_4OH).

In the lists which follow, the chemicals are listed in alphabetical order along with the formula necessary to make the chemical, the procedure to follow in using each chemical and a discussion of the use of each chemical. The usage of each chemical is repeated under chemical reactions in each of the chapters.

A. WETTING AGENTS

Several reagents are used to wet dried material or to remove unwanted air bubbles from the sections. These are as follows:

Ethanol: 70-95% aqueous solution; used to treat dried material so that water can be absorbed by the hyphae. At times mixed with Phloxine to remove air bubbles.

Teepol: When working with fresh material, used to prevent unwanted air bubbles from accumulating in the section.

B. USEFUL COMPANION AGENTS

Acetocarmine
Formula 1(from Grund & Marr, 1965)
a. Reflux 1:1 (v:v) glacial acetic acid and water solution containing an excess of carmine for 6 hours.
b. Mordanting Solution: either A or B
 A. 5% aqueous ferric chloride
  (5 gr. $Fecl_3 \cdot 6H_2O$ in 95 cc H_2O);
 B. 3% ferric ammonium sulfate
  Mix 3 gr. Ammonium sulfate $((NH_4) \cdot SO_4 \cdot 24H_2O)$; 1 ml glacial acetic acid; 0.1 ml conc. sulphuric acid (H_2SO_4). Dilute this mixture to 100 ml with distilled water.

Formula 2 (from Henderson, Orton, and Watling, 1969)
Prepare 45% glacial acetic acid (45 cc Acetic Acid in 55 cc H_2O) and 45% ethanol (45 cc ETOH in 55 cc H_2O). Boil the Acetic Acid with excess of carmine for ½ hour, filter and dilute to half strength with ETOH; add 2-4 drops of ferric hydroxide $Fe(OH)_3$.

Procedure & Use: Basidia of certain agarics, such as species of *Lyophyllum*, contain large particles which turn blackish purple or violet black in acetocarmine. Such basidia are best called **Siderophilous** (although in some texts termed **Carminophilous**).
 Using the Grund & Marr technique submerge a gill piece (usually over 4 mm^2) in 2 ml of mordant solution in a watch glass and boil for approximately 1 minute over a direct flame. Transfer the gill to a second watch glass containing 2 ml of acetocarmine solution and again boil for 1 minute over a direct flame. Transfer a small section of gill into a few drops of a 50% chloral hydrate solution on a glass slide. After covering the section, observe immediately.
 Using the Henderson et. al. technique, place a small piece of gill in a few drops of the liquid on a glass slide and heat over a direct flame. When the liquid begins to evaporate and a film forms, remove the fragment into a few more drops of solution on another glass slide. Repeat two or three times.

Amman's Solution (See Cotton Blue)

Ammonium Hydroxide (NH_4OH): 3-10% aqueous solution.
Formula:
 To prepare the desired percentage solution, dissolve X ml of NH_4OH into 100-X ml (cc) of water. For example, a 10% solution is prepared by dissolving 10.gms of NH_4OH into 90 cc of water. Household ammonia can be substituted for ammonium hydroxide.
Procedure & Use: This chemical is used as a medium into which sections of dried material are placed after wetting with ethanol. Cells swell to near their original size and shape in this solution. Ammonium hydroxide is a good medium to view spore ornamentation and the internal structure of spores; spore color may be altered when viewed in this solution, (e.g. the spores of the *Bolbitiaceae*

23

will darken considerably). Some agaricologists use ammonium hydroxide to demonstrate a plage (e.g. in *Galerina*) by placing the spores in a few drops of this solution after washing them in a 50% aqueous solution of chloral hydrate.

European mycologists prefer ammonium hydroxide (NH_4OH) over the potassium hydroxide (KOH) used by American mycologists since the former chemical will not leave a crystalline residue when the section evaporates whereas the latter chemical will. Furthermore, European mycologists tend to use a 10% solution of ammonium hydroxide whereas American mycologists tend to use a 2.5 to 3.0% solution.

Some other uses of ammonium hydroxide are as follows: to show the chrysocystidia in *Hypholoma, Stropharia*, and *Pholiota*, the trama of *Xeromphalina*, the mucilage caps on the pseudocystidia of *Psathyrella* (a green reaction), the incrusted hyphae of many agarics, the pleuro- and caulocystidia of *Xeromphalina* (red-brown reaction) and the trama of certain *Collybia* spp. (green reaction).

Chloral Hydrate: 50% aqueous solution.
Formula:
   Dissolve 50 gms of chloral hydrate in 50 cc (ml) water.
Procedure & Use: Used as the mounting medium into which pieces of gill tissue are placed after being stained with acetocarmine (see above). Also used as the medium to clear spores in order to view the plage (see ammonium hydroxide).

Chlorovanillin
Formula: (Singer, 1975)
   Dissolve 5 mg vanillin crystals in 2.0 ml (cc) water and 4.0 ml (cc) concentrated hydrochloric acid. Use standard 65% HCl solution; keep vanillin crystals handy. Solution should be made before each usage.
Procedure & Use: See Sulfobenzaldehyde.

Congo Red: 1% aqueous solution; saturated solution in NH_4OH.
Formula 1.
   Dissolve 1 (2) gms of Congo Red in 99 (98) cc water; filter the excess dye.
Formula 2.
   Saturate concentrated Ammonium hydroxide with Congo Red.
Use: Usually used in combination with Phloxine and water (for fresh material) or ammonium hydroxide or potassium hydroxide (for dried material). Congo Red will stain the walls of hyphae whereas Phloxine is used to stain the interior of the hyphae.
Procedure: After reviving the cell, place the material to be studied in a mixture of one drop 1(-2)% Congo Red, 1(-2)% Phloxine, and one drop 3(-10)% ammonium hydroxide or one drop 3(-5)% potassium hydroxide. Remove excess dye by influxing more alkali which can be drawn under the cover slip by placing a piece of absorbent material on one side of the cover slip. In order to improve the contrast of the staining reaction, place a few drops of KOH or NH_4OH on one side of the cover slip and draw the liquid under the cover slip by placing a piece of absorbent material on the opposite side of the cover slip. The excess dye

under the cover slip will dissolve in the KOH or NH_4OH and will be removed by the absorbent material (kleenex, paper towels, etc.). Continue adding KOH or NH_4OH until all the excess dye is removed; the sections will then appear reddish on a colorless background.

Agaricologists have used the saturated Congo Red – Ammonium hydroxide solution to study the spore wall of some agarics, e.g. *Chlorophyllum*, by placing the spore in a drop of this solution and a drop of 5% KOH; the complex spore wall will appear reddish in color.

Cotton Blue (Amman's Solution; Aniline Blue): (Note: the dye, cotton blue is usually used in solution with a mixture of lactic acid and phenol).
Formula: (from Henderson, Orton, and Watling, 1969).
   Dissolve 50 ml of 1% aqueous solution of Cotton Blue (1 gm cotton blue in 99 ml water) in lactic acid (100 gm), phenol (100 gm), glycerine (150 ml), H_2O (50 ml). Some investigators use a 1% lactic acid solution of cotton blue made by dissolving 1 gm of cotton blue in 99 ml lactic acid.
Procedure: Place the material to be studied in one drop of cotton blue on a glass slide; study after covering with a cover slip. The reaction is enhanced by boiling and it may take up to one hour to get a positive reaction.
Use: In certain agarics, e.g. some species of *Lepista*, the spore wall absorbs a greater concentration of cotton blue than does the cytoplasm. Sometimes the ornamentation is more strongly colored than the rest of the spore, e.g. *Gomphus*. When the wall or ornamentation is distinctly contrasted with the inner portion of the spore, the spore is called **Cyanophilous**. Cotton blue can also stain the walls of the hyphae of selected portions of the basidiocarp (as in *Crinipellis*). Furthermore in certain chrysocystidia the contents stain intensely blue in Cotton Blue.

Cresyl Blue: a dilute aqueous solution; try .5 – 1.0%
Formula:
   Dissolve 0.5 – 1.0 gm cresyl blue in 99.5 – 99.0 ml H_2O. Allow to stand for 5-10 minutes then filter out the excess dye.
Procedure: Place the material to be studied in one drop of cresyl blue on a glass slide; study after covering with a cover slip.
Use: Certain spore walls and various hyphae turn reddish to violet when placed in Cresyl Blue. Such a reaction is called **Metachromatism** and the structures reacting positively are called **Metachromatic**. Some examples are: the spores of *Macrolepiota*, the hyphae of the stipe of some species of *Mycena*, gloeocystidia of the *Corticiaceae*, walls of the cystidia of *Melanoleuca*, the trama of many species of *Agrocybe*, the basidia of *Tricholoma*, and the spore ornamentation in certain species of *Russula*. Cresyl Blue is invaluable in locating gelatinized areas of the basidiocarp.

Erythrosin: after Palmer, 1955.
Formula:
   Saturated concentrated Ammonium hydroxide with Erythrosin A.
Use: Invaluable background for non-staining hyaline structures such as the exosporium of certain spores; excellent stain for staining the protoplast within

hymenial elements.

Fuchsin:
Formula:
Strong Carbol Fuchsin; 10% Hydrochloric Acid (HCl).
Procedure: Place the material to be studied in strong Carbol Fuchsin for 15 minutes; wash off with 10% Hydrochloric Acid, leave in the acid for 1 minute. Wash off with water and observe in water.
Use: This chemical is used to distinguish certain types of hyphae and granules especially in the macrocystidia of certain *Russula* sp. A positive reaction is a reddish purple.

Guaiac: saturated solution
Formula:
Prepare a saturated solution of gum guaiacum in 70% ethanol.
Procedure: Place the material to be studied in a drop of guaiac on a prepared slide; study after covering with a cover slip.
Use: Guaiac is normally used as a reagent to study the macrochemical reactions of the basidiocarp. However, it is also used to study the incrusted cystidia of some species of *Inocybe*. (1% aqueous solutions of pyronic acid have been used to replace Guaiac in French studies in this last genus.)

Hydrochloric Acid: (Remember Hydrocholoric Acid is corrosive, so be careful.)
Formula:
Concentrated solution.
Procedure & Use: Place the material in a drop of reagent and cover. This acid is used to distinguish hyphae and cells in certain groups of agarics, such as *Coprinus* and *Cortinarius*; a positive reaction is either green or shades of red. Hydrochloric acid is essential in studies with certain sections of *Coprinus* where it distinguishes between globose veil cells with diverticulae and crystalline debris.

Melzer's Reagent (affectionately known as Melzer's):
Formula:
Add Iodine (1.5 gm), Potassium-Iodide (5.0 gm), and Chloral Hydrate (100 gm(ml)) to H_2O (100 ml). Warm but do not boil.
Procedure: Place the material to be studied in a drop of Melzer's then cover.
Warning: do not mix Melzer's with any type of alkali as a cloudy precipitate will develop immediately. A positive reaction usually occurs immediately but in doubtful cases it is best to leave the material in the solution for 20 minutes. Frequently it's best to turn the light source of the microscope to high in order to enhance the contrast of the reaction.
Use: Three color reactions of material mounted in Melzer's can occur. These are: 1) a blue to black reaction (positive) in which case the material is called **Amyloid**; 2) a brownish to reddish-brown reaction in which case the material is called **Pseudoamyloid** (or **Dextrinoid**); and 3) a yellow to hyaline reaction (neg ative) in which case the material is called **Inamyloid**. Some examples of positive reactions (amyloid) to Melzer's are as follows: spores of some species of *Cystoderma*, spore ornamentations of *Russula* and *Lactarius*, hyphae of *Chro-*

26

ogomphus and septa in some hyphae of certain species of *Boletus*. Examples of the pseudoamyloid reaction are: the spores of *Hygrophoropsis* or *Paxillus panuoides*, the hyphae of certain species of *Mycena*, and the pileus hairs of *Crinipellis*.

Methylene Blue: 1% aqueous solution
Formula:
  Dissolve 1 gm of Methylene Blue (Methyl Blue) in 99 cc water.
Procedure & Use: Same as for Cresyl Blue. Some agaricologists think that the resolution of the hyphal characters is better in this reagent than in Cresyl Blue.

Phloxine: 1% aqueous solution.
Formula: Dissolve 1(-2) gm Phloxine in 99(-98) ml H_2O; filter out the excess dye.
Procedure & Use: Routinely used with Congo Red and an alkali (KOH or NH_4OH) to study all types of hyphae. Phloxine is taken up by the diffused cytoplasm within the hyphae whereas Congo Red is primarily taken up by the walls. For use see Congo Red.

Potassium Hydroxide (KOH): 3-5% aqueous solution
Formula:
  Dissolve 3(-5) gms of potassium hydroxide in 97(-95) ml water.
Procedure: Place the material to be studied in a drop of potassium hydroxide on a glass slide; add Congo Red and/or phloxine if desired.
Use: 3% KOH is the reagent used by most American mycologists to revive the hyphae of dried basidiocarps. For a discussion of the uses of this chemical, see the uses of ammonium hydroxide (NH_4OH).
  Some examples of specific microchemical reactions with potassium hydroxide are as follows: incrustations of certain hyphae turn faintly yellow, internal contents of chrysocystidia turn yellow (as in *Hypholoma*), the pileus hairs of *Crinipellis* turn gray and the hyphae of the pileipellis of certain species of *Cystoderma* turn reddish brown.

Sodium Hydroxide (NaOH): 3(-5)% aqueous solution
Formula: Dissolve 3(-5) gm sodium hydroxide in 97(-95) ml water.
Procedure & Use: Substituted for potassium hydroxide.

Sulphobenzaldehyde (Sulfobenzaldehyde)
Formula: (from singer, 1975).
  Dissolve 6 cc of Benzaldehyde into 3 cc distilled water and 10 cc concentrated (pure) sulphuric acid (H_2SO_4).
Procedure: Place the material to be studied into a few drops of sulphobenzaldehyde. Be careful as the reagent contains sulphuric acid which is highly corrosive.
Use: Darkens the contents of macrocystidia, pseudocystidia, some oleiferous hyphae and some lactiferous hyphae in certain agarics, particularly species of *Russula*. Several chemicals can be substituted for sulphobenzaldehyde, namely chlorovanillin, sulphovanillin, and sulphoformol.

Laticiferous elements of the Russulaceae turn brown in sulphoformol, black in sulfobenzaldehyde and dingy violet to carmine in sulfovanillin and chlorovanillin.

Sulphoformol (Sulfofomol)
Formula:
   Mix 6 cc of a 40% aqueous solution of formaldehyde in 3 cc distilled water and 10 cc concentrated (pure) sulphuric acid.
Procedure & Use: Same as Sulphobenzaldehyde.

Sulphovanillin (Sulfovanillin)
Formula:
   Dissolve 5 mg pure vanillin in 2.0 cc distilled water and 4.0 cc concentrated (pure) sulphuric acid. The acid can be stored separately and just enough crystals added each time to make a yellow liquid.
Procedure & Use: see sulphobenzaldehyde.

Sulphuric Acid: concentrated.
Formula:
   Use material from reagent bottle.
Procedures: Place material to be studied in drop of concentrated sulphuric acid. *Care is absolutely* necessary when working with sulphuric acid as it is extremely caustic.

Toludine Blue: 1% aqueous solution.
Formula:
   Dissolve 1gm Yoludine Blue in 99ml water.
Procedure & Use: see Methylene Blue.

Trypan Blue: (from Dade, in Herb. IMI Handbook, Kew, 1960)
Formula:
   Dissolve 50 ml of a 0.2% aqueous solution of Trypan Blue (5 mg in 250 ml water) in lactic acid (100 gm), phenol (100 gm), glycerol (150 ml), H_2O (50 ml).
Procedure & Use: As with cotton blue, although invaluable for staining the inner layer of the hyphal wall and some spores.

IV. HYPHAE

Agaricologists divide the hyphal system of the basidiocarp into convenient categories. These include the distinctive terminal cells of the hyphae (dermato-cystidia, hymenocystidia, basidia), the characters of constituent hyphae on the surfaces of the basidiocarp (pileipellis, stipitipellis and the hymenium) and the features of contextual hyphae which constitute the trama or flesh of the gills, pileus and stipe. These categories tend to obscure the fact that the entire basidio-carp consists of modified hyphae which are entangled and interwoven. Regard-less of location (pileus, stipe, gills or pores) all hyphae have features in common. Hyphal modifications will be discussed with respect to systemization, wall char-acteristics, septation, branching, inflation, pigmentation and microchemical reaction.

A. HYPHAL SYSTEMS

Hyphae in the basidiocarp can be categorized according to two systems: One, initiated by Corner in 1932 (elucidated by Talbot, 1954) and the other by Fayod in 1889 (enlarged by Singer, 1975).

The Corner system of "hyphal analysis" has been called the **Mitic System**. In this scheme of categorizing hyphae, three systems are described (Talbot, 1954): 1) **Monomitic** —a system composed of **Generative Hyphae** (Fig. 8A) which are thin-walled, branched, narrow (1.5-10μm) and septate. 2) **Dimitic** -a system composed of generative and **Skeletal Hyphae** (Fig. 8B). The latter type hyphae are thick-walled, unbranched, aseptate and straight to slightly flexuous; the lumen is more or less obliterated except sometimes at the apices where the walls are thin and enclose dense contents. 3) **Trimitic** (Fig. 8D) —a system com-

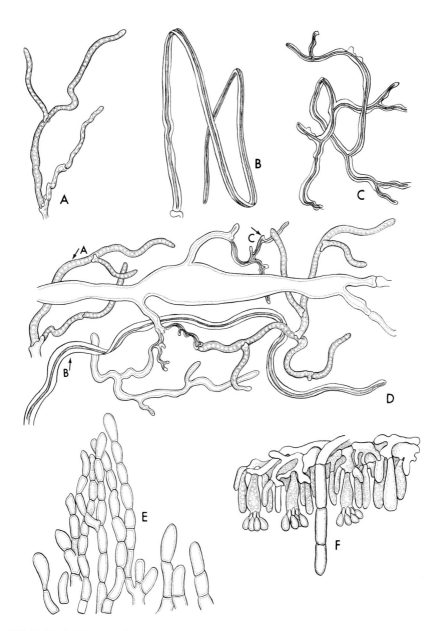

FIG. 8. **Hyphal System. A.**Generative Hyphae; **B.** Skeletal Hyphae; **C.** Binding Hyphae; **D.** Trimitic hyphal system with generative, binding and skeletal elements; **E.** Hyphal Peg of *Lentinus ceasarius;* **F.** Cheilocystidium. A,B,C redrawn from Webster (1970); D redrawn from Corner (1966).

posed of generative, skeletal and **Binding** (or **Ligative**) hyphae. The **Binding** hyphae are defined as thick-walled, distinctly branched and tortuous, and often lack a lumen (Fig. 8C). Bewildering variations of the mitic system have been described, some of which are as follows:

Amphimitic: a system composed of generative and binding hyphae.

Physalomitic: a term applied to any system in which the hyphal cells inflate; therefore you can have physalomonomitic, physalodimitic, physalotrimitic, physaloamphimitic and so on.

Sarcomitic: a term applied to any system in which thin-walled skeletals are present; therefore you can have sarcodimitic or sarcotrimitic hyphal systems.

The system of "hyphal analysis" according to Fayod divides the hyphae of a basidiocarp into two tissues, the **Fundamental** and the **Connective**. Singer adds a third category, the **Conducting** system or tissue. The fundamental tissue is composed of thick-walled skeletal and binding hyphae of the woody fungi, thin or thick-walled sphaerocyst nests, and "inflated multiseptate hyphae with firm walls that are formed in the early development of the carpophore" (Singer, 1975, p. 30). The connective tissue is made of thin-walled hyphae of which the generative hyphae form the major component. The elements of the conducting tissue transport metabolic substances which may be excreted or secreted. Components of the conducting system are such specialized hyphae as laticiferous, oleiferous, gloeovessels, etc.

Most agarics and boleti have a monomitic system as well as the three types of tissues outlined above, i.e. the fundamental, the connective, and the conducting; a few more woody agarics possess a dimitic structure. However, the definitions of these systems are not critical to understanding microscopic features of mushrooms. Singer stated this attitude most admirably as follows: "It is my opinion that, at least in the present stage of our knowledge, it is useless and even dangerous to press the great variety of tramal structures known in the fleshy Basidiomycetes into new rigid terms" . . . and "it is best to merely describe what we see" (1975, p. 31).

B. THE HYPHAL WALL

The wall of hyphae may be **Thin** [not accurately measurable with a compound microscope and usually less than $0.5\mu m$ wide (from Smith, 1966)], or the wall may be **Thick**. In thick-walled hyphae, the wall may be even the length of the cell or it can vary in thickness. Also terminal cells (i.e. cystidia or basidia) can be thick-walled or partially so.

Hyphal walls can be **Incrusted** due to the deposition of various materials (Fig. 9; Pl. I). Such incrustations are generally considered a type of pigmentation, vary in shape and can be found on all hyphae including terminal cells. The wall may also be ornamented with spirals, pimples, spines or pegs. These are considered outgrowths of the wall and are generally restricted to terminal cells. The rod-like wall protrusions of the intercalary (non-terminal cells) cells of *Mycena filopes* (for instance) are an exception (Pl. II C).

Hyphae can be imbedded in a gel (Pl. II D). They are best observed in an alkali (either KOH or NH_4OH) to which either Phloxine and Congo Red or Cresyl Blue have been added. These reagents stain the hyphae quite distinct

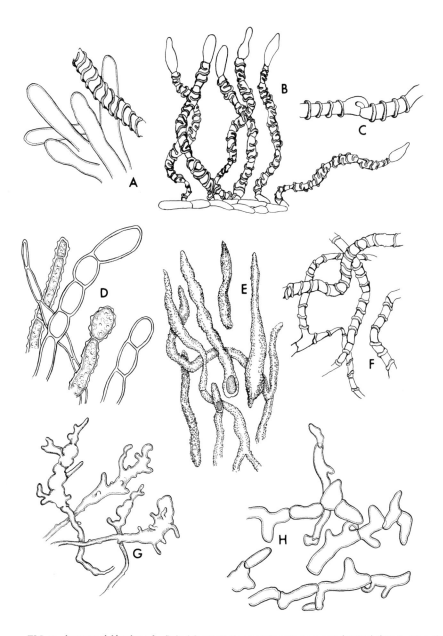

FIG. 9. **Incrusted Hyphae A.** Spiral Incrustations of *Eccilia pungens* (TYPE) (Pileipellis); **B.** Ring-like to more or less Spiral Incrustatuions of *Boletus chrysenteron* (Pileipellis); **C.** Ring-like Incrustations of *Gymnopilus spectabilis* (Pileipellis): **D,** Irregular Incrustation of *Coprinus xanthothrix* (Veil); **E.** Incrusted hyphae of *Suillus brevipes*(Pileus Context); **F.** Ring-like Incrustations of *Ramicola haustellaris* (Pileipellis); **G.** Rod-like Outgrowths of *Mycena epipterygia* (Cheilocystidia); **H.** Short, Rod-like Branches of *Cystoderma* (Part of Pileipellis).

while the gel or mucilage remains colorless; the gel separates the hyphae one from the other. The gel can originate as a breakdown product of the wall itself in which case the hyphae appear very thin and may be completely lost, or it can originate from the interhyphal secretion in which case the hyphae appear to be normal in width.

C. SEPTATIONS

The hyphal strands of a basidiocarp are normally divided into shorter units by cross walls or **Septa** (**Septum**, singular); such hyphae are considered **Septate**. Septa can be formed by rapid cytoplasmic breakdown and restoration of the wall due to the deposition of new wall material, or a construction can form due to depositions along an existing wall. The former type of septum is called a **Cleavage Septum** whereas the latter type is called a **Pseudoseptum**.

Some hyphae of the basidiocarp of agarics and boletes appear to be **Aseptate**, i.e. without a septum. Such hyphae seem to have a supportive or binding function (skeletal or binding hyphae) or they may contribute to conduction or transportation (as in the specialized hyphae of the conducting tissues).

Hyphae sometimes separate (disarticulate) at the septum and may or may not be inflated. Examples of inflated and disarticulated hyphae can be found in the veil of certain *Coprinus* species (Fig. 10D; Pl. III D), and the pileipellis of *Phaeolepiota* (Fig. 10A) or the sphaerocyst nests of *Russula* (Fig. 10B; Pl. III B) or *Lactarius*. An example of a tissue with noninflated, disarticulated hyphae is the pellis of *Leccinum* (Fig. 10E; Pl. II A).

D. HYPHAL BRANCHING

The elements of the connective tissue in agarics and boletes are usually regularly branched, long, and septate whereas the elements of the fundamental tissue remain unbranched. On the other hand, the elements of the conductive tissue are characteristically flexuous and sinuous with irregular branching.

The branches can be long and difficult to observe or short and easy to interpret as in the short branched hyphae of the pileipellis of certain *Coprinus* species. Branches are usually scattered and more often than not a single branch is produced per cell; in paarige branching (found in several boletes) several branches appear at the same level.

A specialized type of hyphal branch which is always associated with a septum and apparently involved with the movement of nuclei within the hypha is called a **Clamp Connection** (Fig. 11A-E; Pl. IV), often telescoped to clamp. Any hypha or hyphal modification (such as cystidia, basidia, etc.) may have a clamp connection. Always check for clamps in the hyphae of the basal tomentum, veils, pileiand stipitipellis and at the base of basidia, basidioles and cystidia.

Not all hyphae possess clamp connections. The negative statement "clamp connections absent" should not be made without a careful search of several locations on several basidiocarps.

An abundance of clamp connections should be noted as this feature has been used to distinguish closely related genera. Moreover the shape of the clamp connection should also be observed. Most clamp connections are quite slender

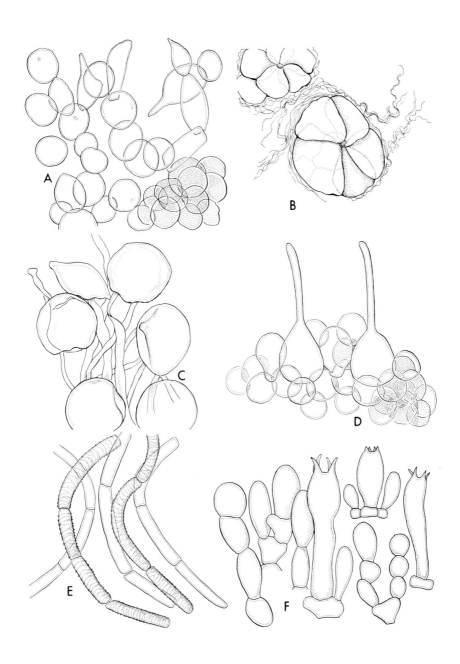

FIG. 10. **Inflated or Disarticulating Hyphae. Cheilocatenulae. A.** Sphaerocytes of *Phaeolepiota aurea* (Pileipellis); **B.** Sphaerocyst nests of *Russula mairei;* **C.** Sphaerocytes of *Amanita aspera* (Veil); **D.** Sphaerocytes of *Coprinus* sp., **E.** Disarticulating, Incrusted hyphae of *Leccinum;* **F.** Cheilocatenulae of *Agaricus* sp.

34

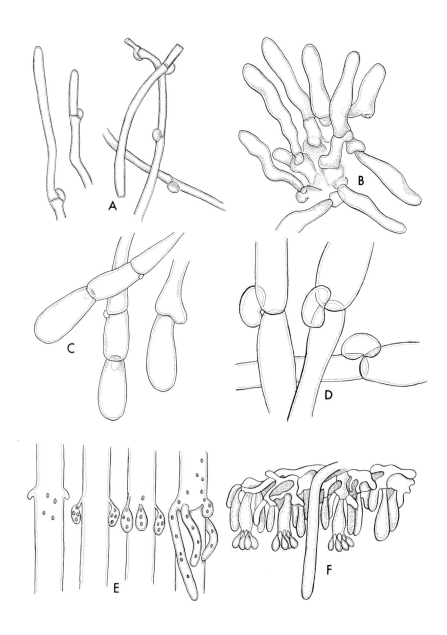

FIG. 11. **Clamps and Cystidioid Hyphae. A.** *Phylloptopsis midulans* (Pileipellis); **B.** *Nolanea sericea* (Base of Basidia); **C.** *Entoloma* sp.; **D.** Medallion Clamp of *Leptonia cyanea* (Pileipellis); **E.** Pseudoclamps of *Coniophora cerebella* (redrawn from Gäumann and Wynd, 1952). **F.** Cystidioid hyphae of *Hygrophorus laetus*.

and rather small; they are very difficult to observe especially when the cells of the clamp inflate and squeeze against other hyphal walls. Some clamp connections, in contrast, are quite large with an obvious gap between the main hypha and the hook connecting the hyphal cells; such clamps are called **Medallion Clamps** (Fig. 11D; Pl. IV D). At times curved branches, which may or may not touch the parent hypha from which they originate, develop and superficially resemble clamp connections. Such structures often develop into branches and then they are called **Pseudoclamps** (Fig. 11E). It is difficult to distinguish these two kinds of branches unless elongation has taken place.

Clamp connections are often difficult to observe. A technique which usually makes clamps easier to see is to stain the hyphae with Congo Red and Phloxine or with Cresyl Blue, Methylene Blue or aqueous Toludine Blue and then splay the hyphae by applying constant but slight pressure to the cover slip with a blunt object such as a pencil eraser or the tip end of a probe. Separating the hyphae improves the contrast between the stained septum and the mounting medium. Phase microscopy greatly assists in ascertaining the presence of a clamp connection as the densely filled curve of the clamp is accentuated by phase optics.

E. HYPHAL INFLATIONS

Any cell, terminal and/or intercalary, of a hypha anywhere in the basidiocarp can be swollen or inflated. Inflated end cells of a hypha when in the hymenium are considered basidia, cystidia or basidioles. The outer surfaces of the basidiocarp, the pileipellis or stipitipellis, may be composed almost entirely of inflated intercalary cells (e.g. *Phaeolepiota aurea* Fig. 10A). They can also make up a part of the context or trama of the basidiocarp.

If an inflated intercalary cell of a hypha appears globose and isodiametric it is called a **Sphaerocyst**. The term sphaerocyst has also been applied to the round, isodiametric cells of some pileipelli (as in *Lepiota*) or to similarly shaped cells of a veil (as in *Amanita* (Fig. 10C; Pl. III C) and *Coprinus* (Fig. 10D; Pl. III D). It is better to use the term **Sphaerocyte** in these instances and restrict sphaerocyst to the components of the nests in *Russula* (Fig. 10B; Pl. III B) and related groups.

When clusters of sphaerocysts are surrounded by ordinary thread-like hyphae, the two kinds of hyphae form what is called **Heteromerous Trama** (hetero= different; merous=parts). If sphaerocysts are absent, the trama remains uniform and is called **Homoiomerous** (homo[io]=same or similar).

F. SPECIALIZED HYPHAE

Laticiferous or *oleiferous hyphae*
The so-called conducting or repository tissues of a basidiocarp are composed of hyphae which are conspicuous due to shape, color, or inclusions. Such specialized hyphae can be traced for long distances throughout the pileus, gill, or stipe tramas. They are septate or aseptate, possess irregularly thickened walls, are often flexuous and/or sinuous, and contain amorphous (granular), possibly resinous or oily, substances. The tips of these specialized hyphae may project into the hymenium and form sterile cells.

Smith (1966) divides these specialized hyphae into **Laticiferous** hyphae or **Laticifers** (or **Lactifers**) if they contain a latex when a basidiocarp is fresh and **Oleiferous** (Pl. II B; III A) hyphae if they do not contain a latex.

Singer divides such hyphae into five types:
1 **Laticiferous Hyphae**: Hyphae that carry latex or are homologous to hyphae containing latex (as in *Lactarius* species).
2. **Oleiferous Hyphae**: Those which carry no latex and often contain a resinous material. Two types exist, those staining with acid-aldehydes (as in *Russula emetica*) and those remaining unchanged (as in *Amanita vaginata*). There may be a correlation of the former type with the acrid taste of basidiocarps.
3. **Gloeo-Vessels**: Vessel-like elements in the trama which are attached to gloeocystidia in the hymenium. These elements are often contorted hyphae which stain deep blue with acid-aldehydes.
4. **Coscinoids**: Highly pigmented conducting elements with an abundance of sieve-like pores in the hyphal surfaces and septa.
5. **Chryso-Vessels**: Hyphae which appear like oleiferous hyphae or gloeo-vessels but contain a granular or resinous material which turns yellow in aqueous alkali solutions.

Cystidia-like hyphae

Certain specialized hyphae project into and beyond the hymenium forming a multicellular "cystidium". Since a cystidium by definition refers to the end cell, reference must be made to these multicellular hyphae. Two such cystidia-like structures are as follows:
Cheilocatenulae (Fig. 10F): Multicellular hyphae which project into the hymenium of the gill edge, the elements of which are in chains (catenulate) and inflated (e.g. in species of *Agaricus, Armillaria mellea, Phylloporus* and *Amanita*).
Cystidioid Hyphae (Fig. 11F): Similar to cheilocatenulae except the elements of the cystidium-like hypha are not differentiated.

G. PIGMENTATION

The types and distribution of pigments in the basidiocarp have assumed a significant role in the taxonomy of the fleshy fungi in recent times. Pigments are extremely varied and can only be identified through complicated chemical procedures. However their distributions are rather easy to determine in the light microscope.

In order to understand the distribution of hyphal pigments, it is necessary to look at the anatomy of a hypha. In the figure below, the following parts of a hypha can be distinguished: cytoplasm, vacuole, a membrane lining the periphery of the hypha, the wall and intercellular spaces.

Pigments are classified according to their distribution as follows:
1. **Cytoplasmic Pigments** are restricted to the cytoplasm. They will appear as a more or less uniform color in the hyphae.
2. **Vacuolar Pigments** are ones restricted to the vacuole and therefore are concentrated in the center of the cell.

3. **Membranal Pigments** or **Intraparietal** pigments occur on the inner portion of the hyphal wall in the form of spirals, rings or irregular clumps. They are not uniform throughout the cell. Furthermore, by carefully focusing the compound microscope, the outer wall of the hypha appears smooth whereas the inner wall or membrane appears ornamented.

4. **Epimembranary Pigments** or **Intercellular Incrustations** form on the outer wall of a hypha and also appear as spirals, rings, pegs or irregular clumps. Since epimembranary pigments are frequently soluble in an alkali, they should be observed in water.

5. **Intercellular Pigments** are found outside the hyphae and thus between the hyphal strands.

6. **Necropigments** are peculiar to the genus *Callistosporium*: They appear as dark inclusions in the contextual hyphae after the basidiocarp body has been dried.

Sections of fresh material should be placed in a concentrated sugar or concentrated salt solution on a prepared slide and covered with a cover slip. The cytoplasm of the hyphae will pull away from the cell wall allowing the contents to be discerned from the wall and hence the pigment distribution.

Dried material should be revived using the alcohol-water method outlined in the technique portion of this book. Once soft, the sections can be viewed in water or an alkali solution. Remember, some pigments, particularly those located in the membrane or wall, are soluble in alkali but not in water: Careful focusing is a must.

Kühner (in Kühner & Romagnesi, 1953) suggests the use of Picroformol of Holland in determining the distribution of pigments. His procedure is described below.

Picroformol of Holland

Formula:

    water . . . . 1,000.0 cc
    neutral copper acetate . . . . .2.5 gms
    picric acid . . . . .4.0 gms
    commercial formalin
      (40% formaldehyde) . . . . 10.0 cc
    glacial acetic acid . . . . 1.5 cc

Procedure & Use:

    a. Crush the copper acetate into a fine powder with a mortar and pestle.
    b. Dissolve the copper acetate in water.
    c. Add the picric acid, little by little, while stirring constantly.
    d. After the picric acid has dissolved, add the formalin and acetic acid.

Technique:

    a. Immerse the tangential sections of lamellae and radial sections of the pileus in picroformol of Holland for at least five minutes.
    b. Immerse the sections in three drops of freshly prepared concentrated chloral hydrate in a watch glass. Place the watch glass over a low flame and bring to the boil.
    c. Observe immediately in concentrated chloral hydrate.

H. CHEMICAL REACTIONS

A discussion of the chemical reagents, their formulae, and procedures to follow can be found on page 22.

The important chemical reagents to use in studying hyphae are Melzer's reagent, Acid-aldehyde compounds (Sulfovanilin, Sulfobenzaldehyde, etc.), Phloxine, Congo Red, Cresyl Blue and Cotton Blue.

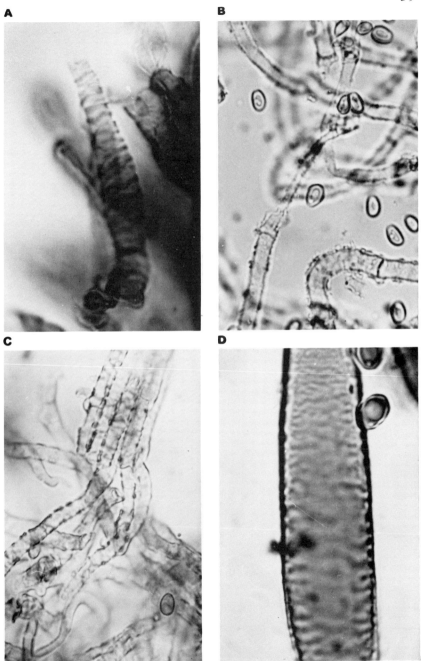

PL. I. **Incrusted Hyphae. A.**_Eccilia pungens_ (pileocystidia); **B.** _Ramicola haustellaris_ (pileus trama); **C.** _Tubaria pellucida_ (pileus trama); **D.** Incrustations on the inner wall of the pileocystidia (_Leptonia zanthophylla_).

40

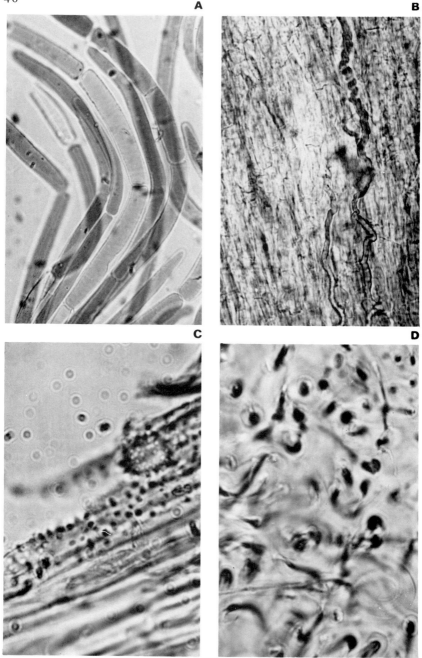

PL. II. **Hyphae 1. A.** Disarticulating Hyphae of the Pileipellis (*Leccinum versipellis*); **B.** Oleiferous Hyphae in the Pileus Trama (*Nolanea* sp.); **C.** Rod-like protrusions on the Pileocystidia (*Mycena idiolens*); **D.** Gelatinized Hyphae in the Pileus Trama (*Hohenbuehlia niger*).

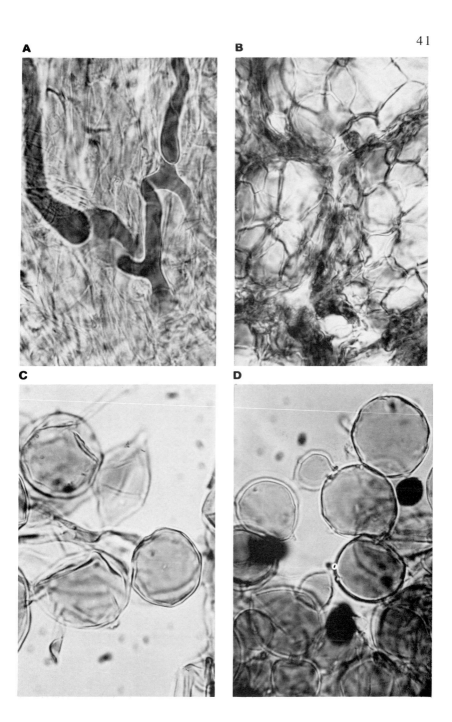

PL. III. **Hyphae 2. A.** Oleiferous Hyphae in the Pileus Trama (*Collybia ansema*); **B.** Sphaerocyst Nests in the Pileus Trama (*Russula mairei*); **C.** Sphaerocytes in the Veil (*Amanita aspera*); **D.** Sphaerocytes in the Veil (*Coprinus niveus*).

42

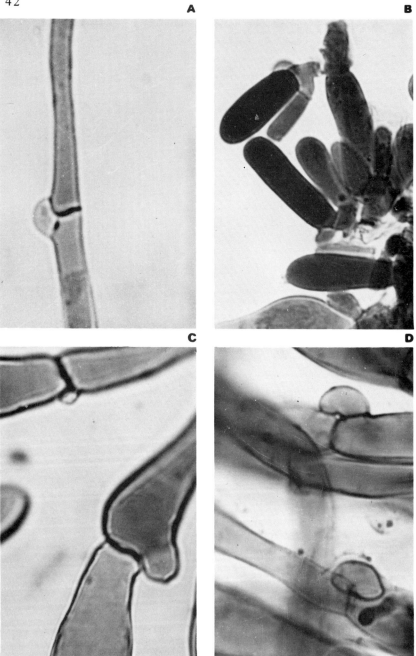

PL. IV. **Clamps A.** Pileocystidia (*Entoloma* sp.); **B.** Base of Basidioles (*Leptonia jubata*); **C.** Pileocystidia (*Agaricus salmoneus*, TYPE); **D.** Medallion Clamps on Pileipellis Hyphae (*Leptonia cyanea*).

V. THE PELLIS OR CORTEX

The outer sterile surface or cortical layer of the basidiocarp is called the **Pellis** (also **Cuticle, Rind**, or **Skin**); the **Pellicle** refers to a viscid pileus from which the cortical layer easily peels off. The pellis of the stipe is called the **Stipitipellis** (or stipe "cuticle") whereas the pellis of the pileus is called the **Pileipellis** (or pileus "cuticle").

The best location to study the pileipellis is at the center or disc of the pileus since it represents the oldest, least disturbed portion of the pileipellis. Radial sections should also be taken halfway to the pileus margin and at the margin itself; these sections should be compared with radial sections from the disc. This comparison will demonstrate the type of pileipellis and any outstanding structural differences in the pileipellis from various parts of the pileus.

European mycholgists prefer the term pellis (and its related terminology) to cuticle which was introduced by Bass (1969). He pointed out that the term cuticle refers only to the non-cellular layer covering the epidermis. However, most American mycologists on the other hand still prefer the term cuticle.

Both longitudinal and cross sections should be made of the stipitipellis at the apex and base of the stipe. If remnants of the partial veil are on the stipe, the same kind of sections should be made just below the veil remnants. In this instance the stipitipellis just below the veil remnants often differs from that at the apex or base of the stipe.

The pellis can be divided up into distinct layers which can be distinguished from the trama; however, it is often very difficult to distinguish the lower limit of the pellis from the upper limit of the trama since hyphae in this region intergrade gradually. For similar reasons it is difficult to differentiate the upper limits of the pellis from the lower limits of the remnants of the universal veil if one is present.

The pellis can be described on the basis of: 1) the layers of the pellis with regard to location; the terms engendered are strictly topographical, 2) the structure and disposition of hyphae in the pellis giving rise to morphological terms, and 3) the elements themselves.

A. TOPOGRAPHY

The pellis of the basidiocarp is composed of layers, the number of which varies with the fungus. If the pellis is composed of just one layer (Fig. 12E), it is called a **Suprapellis**. If two layers (as in Fig. 12B,C) are distinguishable, the outer layer is called the suprapellis and the inner layer next to the pileus trama is called **Subpellis**. If three layers (as in Fig. 12D) can be differentiated, the outer one is called the suprapellis, the middle layer the **Mediopellis**, and the inner layer next to the pileus trama, the subpellis. In those pelli with more than one visible layer, the suprapellis is always the outermost layer and the subpellis is always the layer next to the pileus trama. The subpellis frequently is a pigmented zone just above the pileus trama and is rarely gelatinized. As Bas indicated so well, these terms are strictly topographical and do not imply homology. Thus the suprapellis of one fungus does not necessarily develop in the same manner as the suprapellis of another fungus and therefore the structures can not be compared on a point for point basis.

B. MORPHOLOGY

Terms used to describe the shape of the pellis are usually restricted to the outermost layer, the suprapellis.

The Suprapellis. Descriptive terminololgy of the suprapellis applies to three broad categories including: 1) those which are not distinct from the pileus trama; such a layer is called simply, an **Undifferentiated** suprapellis. 2) those in which the elements are arranged perpendicularly to the surface (ie. anticlinally); such a suprapellis is called a **Derm**. 3) those in which the elements are arranged more or less parallel to the surface (ie. periclinal); such a suprapellis is called a **Cutis**.

Derm. In a derm the elements of the suprapellis are anticlinally arranged and ± parallel to one another as viewed in a tangential or radial section. In a scalp section, a derm appears as a series of thin-walled, oval cells, like so many bubbles.

Variations of a derm are as follows:

Cellular (Cystoderm) (Fig. 13B, C; Pl. V B): The suprapellis is composed of a single row of vesiculose to subglobose to globose cells. Such a layer is also called a monostratous (mono = single, stratous = stratum or layer) cellular suprapellis, or cystoderm (cysto = bag-like).

Epithelium (Polycystoderm) (Fig. 13A; Pl. V A,C): This type of suprapellis is similar to the cellular pellis in that the elements are highly inflated, however, they are in many-layered (pluristratous) chains.

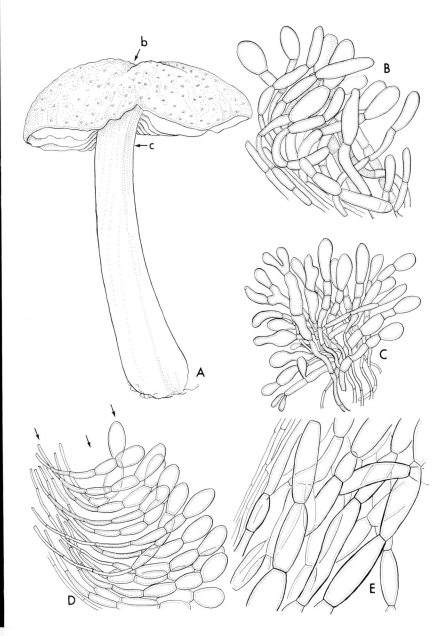

diagrammed from point b on the basidiocarp; C, two layered stipitipellis
diagrammed from point c on the basidiocarp;

; **B.** Two-layered Pileipellis
ered Pileipellis of *Leptonia*
e pileus trama from *Nolanea*

46

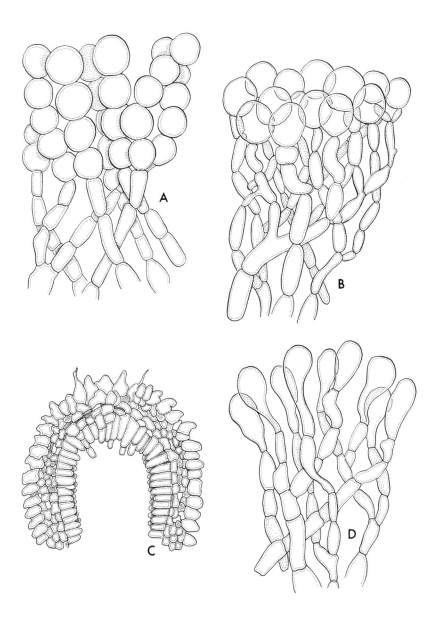

FIG. 13. **Types of Suprapellis (Pileipellis) I. A.** Epithelium or Polycystoderm of *Cysto-derma granulosum;* **B.** Cellular or Cystoderm of *Psathyrella;* **C.** Cellular or Cystoderm with differentiated pileocystidia of *Coprinus* (from a prepared silde); **D.** Hymeniform layer of *Agrocybe erebia.*

Hymeniderm (Pl. IX C): The elements of the suprapellis are exactly like the elements of the hymenium, including basidia. If it lacks functional basidia or cells resembling basidia in morphology and size it is then called a **Hymeniform Layer** (Fig. 13D; Pl. V D).
Palisadoderm (Palisoderm) (Fig. 14A, 15D; Pl. VI A): The terminal elements in this type of derm all reach the same level and form a palisade of inflated, somewhat elongate cells.
Trichoderm (Fig. 14C,D; Pl. VI C,D): In a trichodermium, the ± filiform elements are unequal in length but are still arranged anticlinally. Furthermore, the elements are not strictly parallel but intertwine. If the terminal elements reach more or less the same level, the type of derm is usually described as a **Trichodermial Palisade** (Fig. 14B; Pl. VI B).

The categories described above are not mutually exclusive. For example, in *Psathyrella* (Pl. IX A) there are some species with a cellular cuticle (monostratous or pluristratous) in which the terminal elements are not strictly globose; in these the derm approaches a palisadoderm. In species of *Conocybe* (Pl. IX C) the terminal cells of the monostratous cellular derm can appear similar in shape to basidia and therefore the derm approaches a hymeniderm. Also, in *Leptonia* subgenus *Paludocybe* the suprapellis is a trichodermial palisade on the disc but because of the lateral expansion of the subpellis and cessation of growth in the suprapellis, it becomes ± periclinally oriented in the middle yet repent at the margin (Pl. IX D). There are always examples of intermediates within our artificial system. Thorough descriptions are preferable even though they may involve more than one term.

Any of the type of derms can be composed of gelatinized hyphae. When this occurs the prefix **Ixo** (= sticky or viscid) is placed before the term. Hence the following terms exist: **Ixohymeniderm, Ixopalisadoderm, Ixotrichoderm** (Pl. VIII C).

Cutis (Fig. 16C): A cutis is a generalized term in which the elements of the suprapellis are periclinally arranged. In a tangential or radial section elements of a cutis appear parallel to those of underlying layers. In a scalp section, a cutis looks like a mixture of entangled filaments parallel to the plane of the slide (ie. periclinal). Two general categories of cutis exist. In one the elements are radially arranged from the disc to the margin of the pileus and are parallel to one another. In the other type of cutis the elements are neither parallel to one another nor radially arranged. The first is called a **Parallelocutis** (Pl. VII C) or the **Confluens**-type of cutis since it is found in *Collybia confluens*. The second is called a **Mixtocutis** (Fig. 15B; Pl. IX B) or the **Dryophila**-type of cutis since it is found in *Collybia dryophila*. In a good radial section, the parallelocutis will appear as a layer of ± parallel hyphae whereas the mixtocutis will appear as a layer of entangled hyphae which at times can be fairly thick. If the elements of a cutis inflate, the suprapellis can be called an **Enterocutis** (Fig. 15A,C; 17C,D; Pl. VII D; IX D).

Furthermore, any or all of the elements can be gelatinized and the prefix **Ixo**- can be applied to cuticular terminology, eg. **Ixocutis, Ixoparallelocutis, Ixomixtocutis, Ixoenterocutis**.

Unusual types of PVW. All land there unusual types (and probably many more) of published material below

48

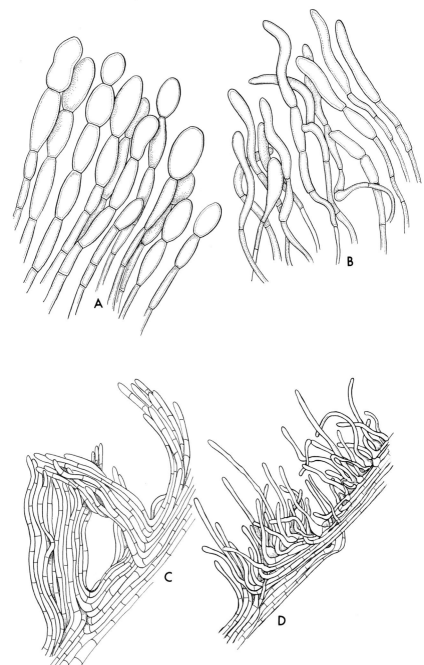

FIG. 14. **Types of Suprapellis. A.** Palisadoderm of *Leptonia avellaneosquamosa* (Pileipellis); **B.** Trichoderminal Palisade of *Leptonia aethiops* (Pileipellis); **C.** Trichodermium of *Leptonia perfusca* (Pileipellis); **D.** Trichodermium of *Leptonia corvina* (Stipitipellis).

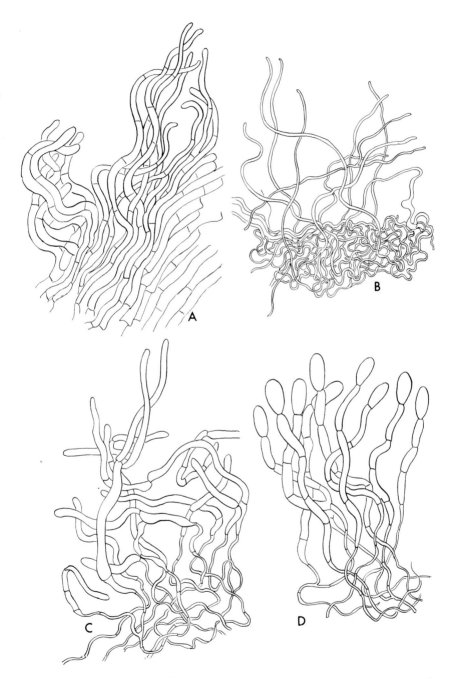

FIG. 15. **Types of Suprapellis (Pileipellis) II. A.** Enterocutis of *Alboleptonia sericella;* **B.** Mixtocutis of *Mycena pura;* **C.** Enterocutis of *Entoloma* sp.; **D.** Palisadoderm of *Leptonia fulva.*

The **Dichophysoid Structure** (or **Asterostromelloid**): This type of pellis is found in *Resupinatus* sensu Singer and is composed of swollen terminal elements with short approximately perpendicular branches. This pileipellis is also reminiscent of that described for *Vararia* in the Aphyllophorales.

Rameales Structure (Fig. 16A,B; Pl. VII A): A type of pellis in which the hyphae of the suprapellis are basically periclinal but possess short vertical branches (as in some species of *Mycena* in which case it is termed **Diverticulate**). The hyphae can also branch irregularly (nodulose, forked, coralloid, etc.) as in species of *Marasmius* section *Rameales*, *Coprinus* subsection *Alachuani*, and *Xeromphalina*.

Dense Structure (Pl. VII B): This type of pellis is essentially an undifferentiated but denser layer of the pileus trama. An example of this can be found in *Lentinus tortulosus*.

Mediopellis and Subpellis: The elements of the mediopellis and/or the subpellis may be arranged periclinally or anticlinally with respect to the hyphae of the pileus trama. Anticlinal elements are usually more parallel and less intertwined in those layers furthest from the pileus trama and become increasingly more intertwined nearer the pileus trama.

C. ELEMENTS OF THE PELLIS

Some terminal cells of the pileipellis and stipitipellis may be differentiated from the surrounding elements in which case the cells are called **Dermatocystidia**.

Although the elements of the mediopellis and the subpellis can do so, those nearest the suprapellis (ie. the outermost) have a greater tendency to gelatinize and to inflate than the elements of the inner layers near the pileus trama. The hyphae of the mediopellis and subpellis can vary from slightly to strongly inflated giving these layers a more or less cellular appearance. Examples of a cellular mediopellis or subpellis can be found in *Hypholoma*, in *Lactarius hygrophoroides* or in species of *Nolanea* and *Mycena* (Fig. 16C; Pl. IX B).

In many species of agarics the elements of the pellis are laterally agglutinated (stuck together) into clumps which compose distinct scales or fibrils on the pileus or stipe. In several genera, (e.g. *Crinipellis*) the laterally agglutinated hyphae form a hair-like strand which is called simply a **Hair (Hair-like Hyphal Strand**, or a **Pilose Agglutination)** (Fig. 17A; Pl. VIII A,B). The hairs form a pilose surface as seen under a hand lens.

An unusual type of pellis (pilei- or stipiti-) element is called a **Ciliate Dermatocystidium** (Fig. 17B) (Singer, 1975) found in various species of *Russula* (eg. *virescens*) and *Lactarius* (section *Plinthogali*). The ciliate dermatocystidium consists of a few basal cells which are short-cylindric or sphaerocyst-like and which end in one or more terminal cells that are subulate or cylindric to rarely clavate and possess an obtuse or acute tip.

The shape, morphology, origin, function, type of pigmentation and the chemical reactions of the dermatocystidia of the pileus (the pileocystidia) and the stipe (the caulocystidia) are discussed on pages 71-81. Terminal elements can

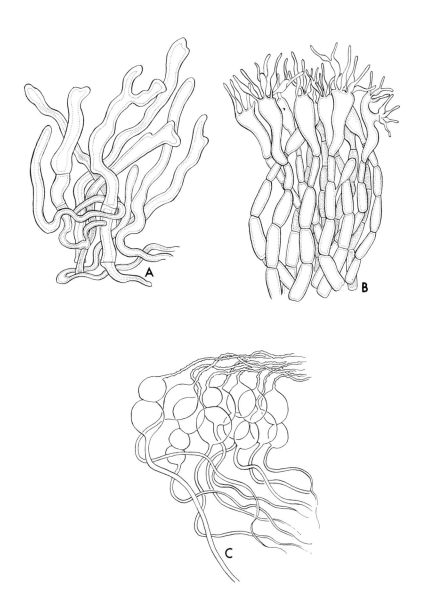

FIG. 16. **Types of Pellis II. A.** Rameales Structure of *Xeromphalina cauticinalis* (Stipiti-pellis); **B.** Rameales Structure of *Marasmius plicatilis* (Pileipellis); **C.** Cutis with a cellular subpellis of *Mycena sanquinolenta* (Pileipellis).

52

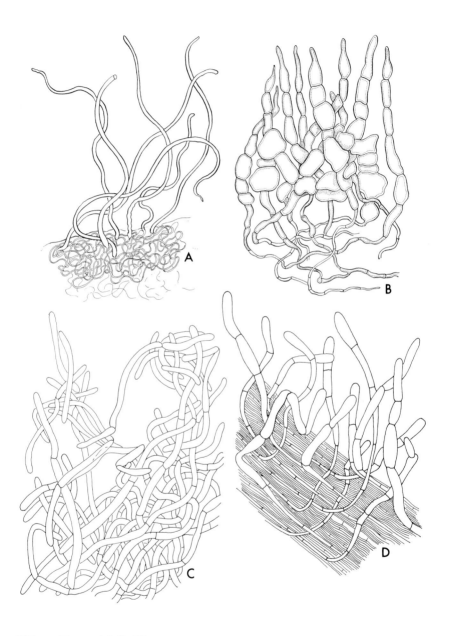

FIG. 17. **Types of Pellis III. A.** Hair-like Hyphal Strand of *Crinipellis piceae;* **B.** Rameales Structure of *Marasmius plicatilis* (Pileipellis); **C.** Enterocutis with a similar Pileus Trama of *Pouzarella versatilis;* **D.** Enterocutis with narrow hyphae of the Stipe Trama from *Pouzarella babingtonii* (Stipitipellis) FIG. 17 (PAGE 52)

B. should read - Ciliate Dermatocystic
(Pileipellis) of Lactarius fuliginosus

vary as to wall thickness and may or may not have clamp connections; these items are discussed on pages 30-35.

D. VEILS

Microscopically, it is possible to differentiate remnants of the universal veil from the adjacent stipitipellis or pileipellis. A radial section of the pileus and a longitudinal section of the stipe base will reveal the veil remnants as a layer of entangled hyphae overlying the pellis.

The remnants of the partial veil can be located on the margin of the pileus or as a ring of tissue around the stipe. As with remnants of the universal veil, the partial veil is sometimes difficult to differentiate from the underlying pellis. Macroscopically partial veils remnants are homogeneous (eg. *Inocybe*) or ultimately become double (eg. some *Cortinarius* spp.); microscopic study of these veil remnants will reveal a similar difference.

The following examples demonstrate the variability of the hyphae of the veils. The floccose veil remnants of *Amanita strobiliformis* (Fig. 18A) are composed of two coequal elements, sphaerocytes and narrow hyphae whereas those of *Amanita cinereoconia* (Fig. 18B) are composed of chains of sphaerocytes which obscure the filamentous hyphae. The veil remnants of *Amanita thiersii* (Fig. 18C) are mostly composed of inflated, clavate cells interspersed with filamentous hyphae. In *Cortinarius*, particularly the subgenus *Myxacium*, the partial veil in the mature basidiocarp is double. The outer veil is composed of gelatinized hyphae whereas the inner veil consists of filamentous, thin-walled, non-gelatinized hyphae.

The veil in *Coprinus* may consist of globose to ellipsoid cells (sphaerocytes) (eg. Sect. *Vestiti*), filamentous cells (eg. Sect. *Impexi*) or sausage-shaped cells (eg. Sect. *Lanatuli*). They may be thick- or thin-walled in each section depending on the species. In the first section the cells may be warted with crystalline material soluble in hydrochloric acid (eg. *C. patouillardii*) or with diverticulae insoluble in this acid (eg. *C. tuberosus*).

E. PIGMENTATION

The elements of the pellis can be distinctly colored due to intracellular, intercellular, epimembranary or encrusted pigments. These pigments should be observed first in water since many are unstable in aqueous alkali solutions. The more stable encrusted or epimembranary pigments can be studied with various chemical reagents and occur as plates, spirals, granules or annular thickenings on the hyphae.

F. CHEMICAL REACTIONS

The chemical reagents used in studying the elements of the pellis are identical to those used in studying hyphae in general, namely Melzer's reagent, acid-aldehyde compounds, aqueous alkali solutions to which Congo Red or Phloxine can be added, Cresyl Blue and Cotton Blue.

The formulae and the procedures to follow for these chemical reagents can be found on page 23.

54

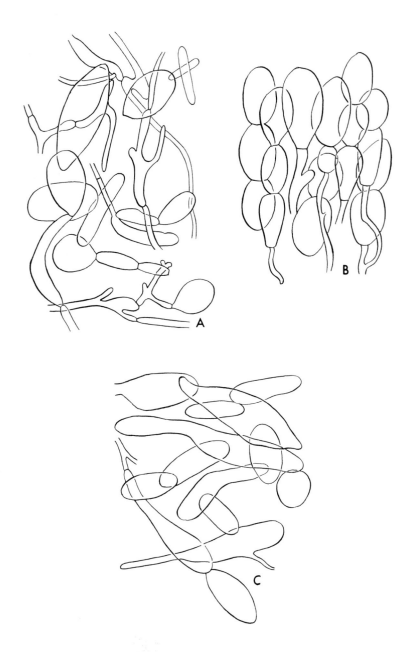

FIG. 18. **Veils. A.** *Amanita strobiliformis;* **B.** *Amanita cineroconia,* **C.** *Amanita thiersii.* (redrawn from Bas, 1969).

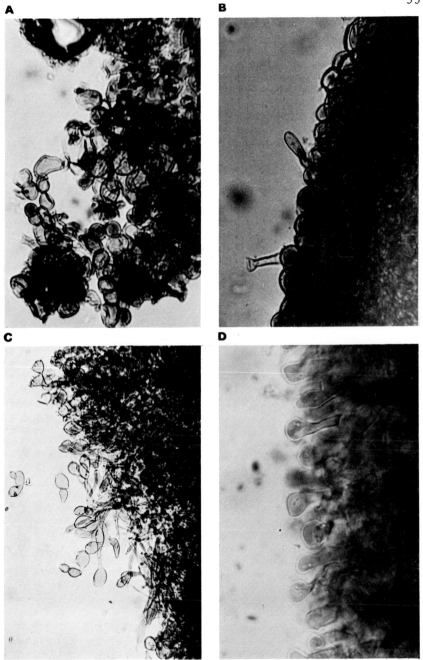

PL. V. **Pileipellis: Derm 1. A.** Epithelium (*Cystoderma granulosum*); **B.** Cellular (*Psathyrella* sp.); **C.** Epithelium (*Phaeolepiota aurea*); **D.** Hymeniform Layer (*Agrocybe erebia*).

56

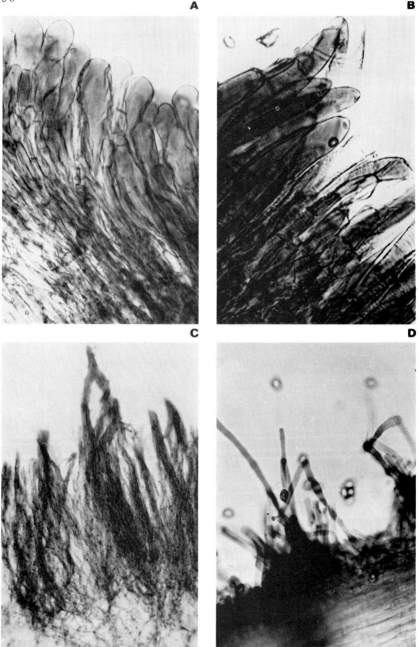

PL. VI. **Pileipellis: Derm 2. A.** Palisadoderm (*Leptonia fulva*); **B.** Trichodermial Palisade (*Leptonia aethiops*) **C.** Trichoderm (*Paxillus atrotomentosus*); **D.** Trichoderm (*Leptonia corvina*).

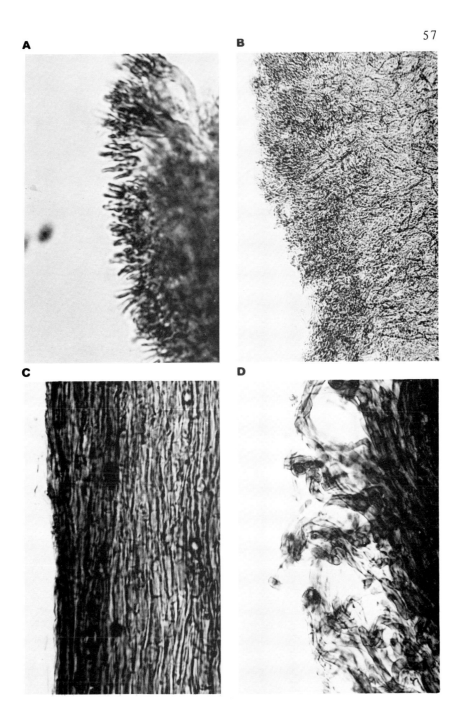

PL. VII. **Pileipellis. A.** Rameales Structure (*Marasmius plicatilis*); **B.** Dense Structure (*Lentinus tortulosus*); **C.** Parallelocutis (*Entoloma* sp.); **D.** Enterocutis (*Alboleptonia sericella*).

58

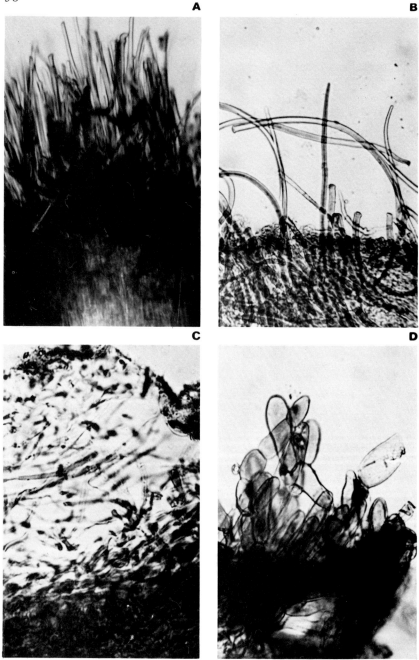

PL. VIII. **Pileocystidia and Pileipellis A.,B.** Hair-like Hyphal Strand (*Crinipellis piceae*); **C.** Ixotrichoderm (*Entoloma madidum*); **D.** Moniliform Hyphae in the Pileipellis (*Leptonia cyanea*).

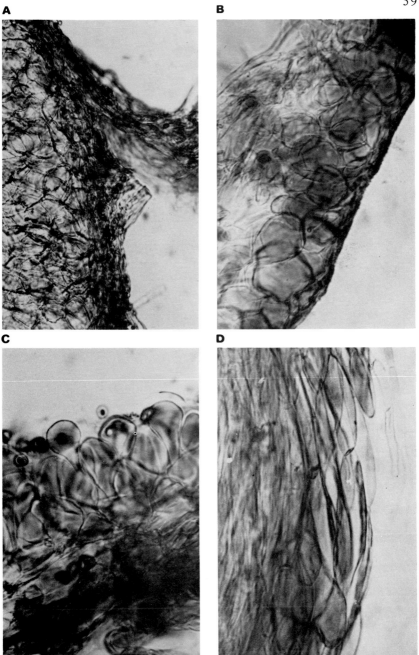

PL. IX. **Pileipellis** A. Hyphae composing the scales overlain on the cellular pileipellis (*Psathyrella velutina*); **B.** Mixtocutis on a cellular layer in the pileus trama (*Mycena subsanquinolenta*); **C.** Hymeniferm (*Conocybe togularis*); **D.** Enterocutis at the Pileus Margin (*Entoloma modestum* TYPE).

PL. IX (PAGE 59)

C. Hymeniderm

VI. TRAMA

The inner portion of a basidiocarp is called the trama (or context) which is topographically distinct from the outer surfaces, the pellis ("cuticle") and the hymenium. The context is divided into three different regions, the hymenophoral trama, the pileus trama, and the stipe trama.

A. HYMENOPHORAL TRAMA (CONTEXT)

The spore-bearing surface (the **Hymenium**) of a basidiocarp overlays sterile tissue which is called the **Hymenophore** (hymeno = hymenium and -phore = to bear). Macroscopically, the hymenophore may assume the form of gills or tubes. Beneath the hymenium is the **Hymenophoral Trama** which in the case of gilled fungi is commonly called **Gill Trama** whereas in the boletes it is called the **Tube Trama**.

The general organization of the hymenophoral trama can be determined by making a tangential slice of the pileus through the hymenophore. The result is a wedge-shaped view of several adjacent gills or a longitudinal section of the tubes, in agarics and boletes respectively. The cut should be as nearly vertical as possible since a slight variance from this plane will make it difficult to interpret the organization of the hyphae of the hymenophoral trama, particularly in the boletes. After the initial cut, thin sections should be made parallel to the plane of the cut in the manner outlined in the technique portion of this book. The initial section should be rather thick so that it can be observed under a dissecting scope or a good hand lens. By viewing at low power the general organization of the hymenophoral trama can be determined. Subsequent thin sections should be mounted in the desired reagent and observed under a compound microscope in order to clarify the organization of the hyphae. Features of the hymenophoral trama will be obscured if the sections are too thick or if the sections are not perpendicular to the hymenophore.

The hymenophoral trama usually consists of two layers, a narrow zone of small, short hyphae immediately beneath the hymenium which is called the **Subhymenium** and the **Hymenophoral Trama Proper**.

1. Hymenophoral Trama Proper

The **Hymenophoral Trama Proper** consists of hyphae which project downwards from the pileus; the manner in which these hyphae are arranged is considered taxonomically significant by agaricologists.

Arrangement of the hymenophoral trama proper: The construction of the hymenophoral trama proper in the mature basidiocarp has been classified into broad patterns: 1) **Parallel** to **Subparallel** (or regular to subregular), 2) **Interwoven** (or irregular), 3) **Divergent** (or bilateral), and 4) **Convergent** (or inverse).

Parallel to subparallel (or regular to subregular): In this type, the hyphae are arranged parallel to one another in which case the hymenophoral trama proper is said to be *parallel* (regular) (Pl. X B; XI C,D). If the hyphae are mostly parallel to one another and slightly intertwined the trama is said to be *subparallel (subregular)* (Pl. XI A). The hyphal cells which compose tramal tissue may be elongate and cylindrical as in *Hygrophorus conicus* (Fig. 20D) or more or less barrel-shaped as in many species of *Naucoria* or *Tubaria* (Fig. 20E; Pl. XI C).

Interwoven (Irregular) (Fig. 19A; Pl. XI B): In this type, hyphae are intricately entangled as they project downward from the pileus so that the hymenophoral trama proper is said to be *interwoven* (or *irregular*) (eg. *Marasmius oreades*). The hyphal cells are often short, very curved and may or may not be isodiametric.

Bilateral (Divergent) (Fig. 19C,D; Pl. X A,D): In this type, the hyphae project downward from the pileus to from a central strand of parallel or subparallel hyphae from which other hyphae diverge in an oblique fashion. These diverging hyphae run all the way to the subhymenium and thereby "fill up" the remaining portion of the gill. The central strand of *divergent* hymenophoral trama proper, called the *mediostratum*, can be composed of a single column of cells. The two divergent zones which flank both sides of the mediostratum are termed *lateral strata* (hence, bilateral trama) (Pl. X A). The divergent trama is evident at an early stage in the developing basidiocarp (primordium) both in the boleti and gilled fungi. It generally remains intact in the mature basidiocarp. However, in some agarics (eg. *Leucocoprinus*) a slight divergence can be seen in the primordium which later is rapidly lost with maturity.

Bilateral trama has often been classified with or as an alternative for a divergent trama. This is not strictly true as a bilateral trama is applied to a trama which was originally regular and becomes bilateral by inflation whereas divergent applies to a trama which is composed of non-inflated hyphae from the beginning. Bilateral hymenophoral trama can be classified by the type of hyphae of which it is composed. In many species of *Amanita* (Pl. X A) most of the hyphal cells are rather broad, somewhat rectangular, moderately long, and of

62

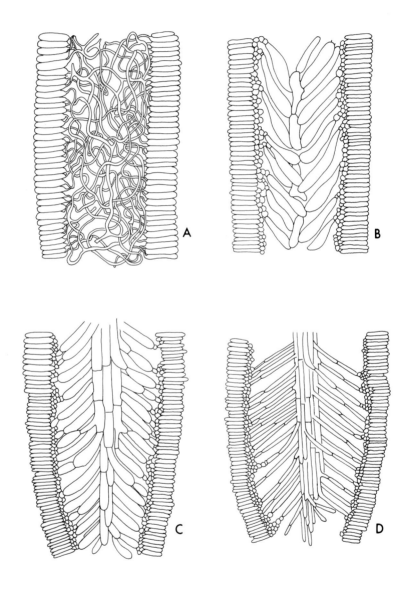

FIG. 19. **Arrangement of the Hymenophoral Trama. A.** Interwoven (*Hygrophorus praetensis*); **B.** Convergent (*Pluteus cervinus*); **C.** Divergent (*Amanita muscaria*); **D.** Divergent (*Hygrophorus bakerensis*). (A,B,C. redrawn from Smith, 1949).

unequal diameter throughout their length. Furthermore, a mediostratum is quite evident. In the second type, as found in *Catathelasma*, the cells of the hyphae are all long, narrow, and isodiametric. The mediostratum is quite reduced and for all practical purposes, not evident. *Convergent (Inverse)* (Fig 19B; Pl. X C): In this type of hymenophoral trama, the hyphae appear to converge toward the center of the trama. Such a hymenophoral trama is called *convergent* (or inverse) and appears to consist of a series of V's. The hyphae of a convergent hymenophoral trama are all quite wide and long. The mediostratum is evident in young tissues but disappears in age.

2. Hymenopodium

In several species of agarics, a distinct zone exists between the hymenophoral trama proper and the subhymenium, called a **Hymenopodium**. In the divergent trama, the hymenopodium lies between the lateral stratum and the subhymenium. However, if the trama is parallel, subparallel or interwoven, the hymenopodium lies between the trama proper and the subhymenium.

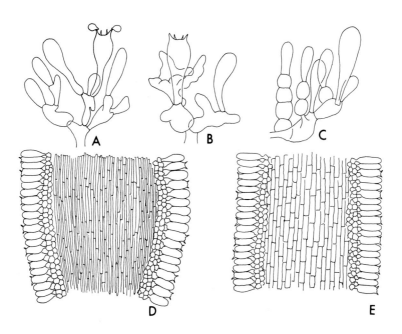

FIG. 20. **Subhymenium and Arrangement of the Hymenophoral Trama Subhymenium: A.** Inflated-Ramose (*Amanita polypyramidis*); **B.** Coralloid (*Amanita sublutea*); **C.** Cellular (*Amanita hongoi*) (redrawn from Bas, 1969). Arrangement of the Hymenophoral Trama; **D.** Subparallel (*Hygrophorus conicus*); **E.** Parallel (*Tubaria* sp.). (redrawn from Smith, 1949).

Although the hymenopodium may be extremely difficult to distinguish from the subhymenium, it is best developed in the following: interwoven (irregular) in some species of *Paxillus* (Pl. XII B) and *Gomphidius*, regular (parallel) and of broad hyphae in *Conocybe* (Pl. XI D), in a thin, regular zone bordering the subhymenium in some species of *Russula* or *Mycena*, and gelatinized in some *Pholiota* spp (Fig. 21 A,C; Pl. XII A).

3. Subhymenium (Fig. 21 D; Pl. XI A,C).

The subhymenium is a topographically distinct region of tissue from which the hymenial elements originate. It is rather uniform consisting of a narrow intertwined hyphae which are smaller, shorter, and much more branched than the basidia and hymenial cystidia which are directly above. This normal type of subhymenium is called **Ramose**. Sometimes the subhymenium is well developed and up to two times wider than the hymenium (eg. in *Amanita* or *Pleurotus* sensu stricto) or the elements themselves are unusual.

Some examples of different subhymenia are ones in which the cells inflate and branch, termed **Inflated-ramose** (eg. *Amanita polypyramidis*) (Fig. 20A); ones in which the cells are shaped irregularly with many projections which do not connect to other cells, termed a **Coralloid** subhymenium (eg. *Amanita sublutea*) (Fig. 20B), or ones in which the cells are ellipsoid to ± isodiametric and the subhymenium is called **Cellular** (eg. *Amanita hongoi*) (Fig. 20C).

Where the hymenium is continuous between adjacent gills it is usually accompanied by a subhymenium. It is at the top of these interlamellar spaces that the subhymenium becomes intricately interwoven with the hyphae of the pileus trama. In some instances, the hymenophoral trama proper also infiltrates the region above the lamellar spaces, creating another layer between the pileus trama and the subhymenium. If the hymenophoral trama is divergent, parallel hyphae of the mediostratum interpose between the interwoven hyphae of the pileus trama and the subhymenium. As a consequence, it is easy to separate the hymenophore from the pileus. Examples of an easily separable hymenophore are found in the Boletaceae and the genus *Paxillus*.

4. The Hyphae of the Hymenophoral Trama

Hyphae of the hymenophoral trama can be as variable as the hyphae in the pileus or stipe. Most hymenophoral tramas consist of thin walled, hyaline hyphae which are narrow and roughly isodiametric.

In species of *Xeromphalina, Marasmius, Lentinus* and *Pleurotus* (basically those which are tough in consistency and revive well when moistened), some hyphae of the trama and hymenopodium are thick walled, rigid and rather large. In contrast the hymenophoral trama in *Russula* is characterized by round, thin-walled cells (sphaerocysts) (Pl. III B) interspersed among flexuous, thread-like hyphae. In *Amanita*, inflated cells are also interspersed among hyphae more typical of the genus. Cells of the hymenophoral trama of *Conocybe* are also of two types — thin, typical ones occupying the mediostratum and broad, short ones on either side. (In *Conocybe* some agaricologists consider these broad later-

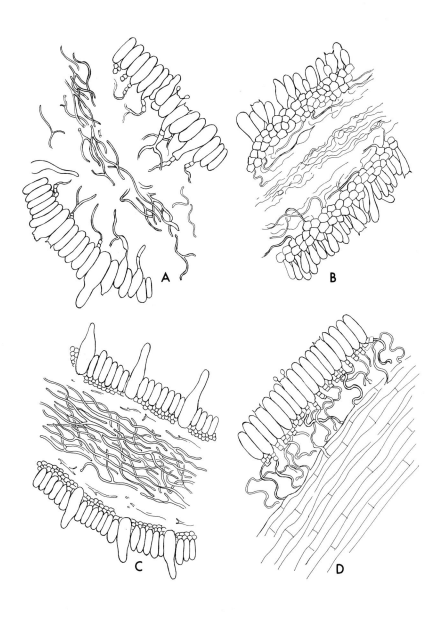

FIG. 21. **Gelatinized Gill Trama. A.,C.** Gelatinized Hymenopodium in *Pholiota decorata* (A, mature; C, young); **B.** Gelatinized Mediostratum in *Paxillus involutus;* **D.** Gelatinized Subhymenium (schematic) in *Entoloma* sp.

66

al cells to be the hymenopodium. (Pl. XI D)). In the above instances the hymenophoral trama is composed of two types of hyphae (excluding oleiferous or laticiferous hyphae which are considered part of the normal hymenophoral trama), and is called **Intermixed**. This term is usually restricted to interwoven, parallel or subparallel tramas but it seems its use can be applied to any type of hymenophoral trama.

Any hypha of the hymenophore trama (the subhymenium, hymenopodium, or trama proper) can gelatinize (Fig. 21A-D; Pl. XI A,C,D; Pl. XII A,B). For example, just the hymenopodium (or subhymenium depending on whose concept you follow) gelatinizes as in some species of *Pholiota* (Fig. 21A,C; Pl. XII A) and *Hygrophorus* (eg. those in the subsection *Laetae* of the section *Hygrocybe*) whereas the entire trama can gelatinize as in *Resupinatus*.

5. Concluding Remarks

The organization of the hymenophoral trama can vary markedly at all developmental stages of the basidiocarp, including the primordium and button stages to an over mature basidiocarp in which almost all of the spores have been formed (and discharged?). For example, in *Phylloporus* the gill trama is divergent until most of the spores form but it becomes parallel to subparallel (or regular to subregular) thereafter. Ordinarily most species descriptions and key choices overlook the stages of basidiocarp development which is considerably important to the disposition of hymenophoral trama. Furthermore, the hymenophoral trama can appear different in fresh and dried specimens. For example, the divergent gill trama of *Hygrophorus bakerensis* (Fig. 19C; Pl. X D) is easily discernible in fresh material but upon drying the tramal hyphae straighten out.

B. THE PILEUS AND STIPE TRAMA

The pileus trama is located between the pileipellis and the subhymenium (ie. above the gills and above the stipe trama). Hyphae of the pileus trama branch downward to form the hymenophoral trama. Although the stipe trama is continuous with the pileus trama an imaginary line conveniently separates the stipe from the pileus. Below this line the hyphae of the stipe trama run more or less longitudinally yet they frequently intertwine.

The stipe trama of most agarics has been insufficiently studied (Pl. XII C,D). However, many tramas are composed of typical thread-like hyphae interlaced with laticifers, oleiferous hyphae, or sphaerocysts. An unusual stipe trama exemplified by several species of *Amanita* (eg. *A. citrina* and *A. porphyria*) is composed of two types of elements: enormous, clavate hyphae and narrow, branching, longitudinally arranged, intertwined hyphae.

The hyphae of the pileus and stipe trama can vary in the following ways: the thickness of the wall, the type of branching, the presence or absence of clamp connections and their presumed functions. Additionally they can possess a variety of pigments, and can react with different chemical reagents. All of these variations are discussed under the heading hyphae on pages 28–43.

C. PIGMENTATION

In many species of agarics and boleti, the trama is distinctly colored because of intracellular, intercellular, epimembranary, or encrusted pigments which react with different reagents. The intracellular pigments are mostly unstable in alkali — while the more stable encrusted or epimembranary pigments are manifested as plates, spirals, granules or annular thickenings on the tramal hyphae. In those forms with intercellular pigments, for example *Cortinarius sanguineus*, the alkali dissolves the pigments and diffuses them throughout the section. In other agarics pigments react with an alkali (KOH) and turn a characteristic color (eg. in *Chroogomphus tomentosus*, pigments become red).

Several types of specialized hyphae can be distributed throughout the trama including endocystidia, oleiferous hyphae and laticiferous hyphae. These are discussed under cystidia or hyphae in other sections of this book.

D. CHEMICAL REACTIONS

Several chemicals are used in studying the trama. These are *Melzer's reagent*, *cresyl blue*, and *acid-aldehydes*. The reactions of the hyphae with these chemicals are discussed on pages 22-28. The hyphae are typically studied in an aqueous alkali solution to which Phloxine or Congo Red can be added.

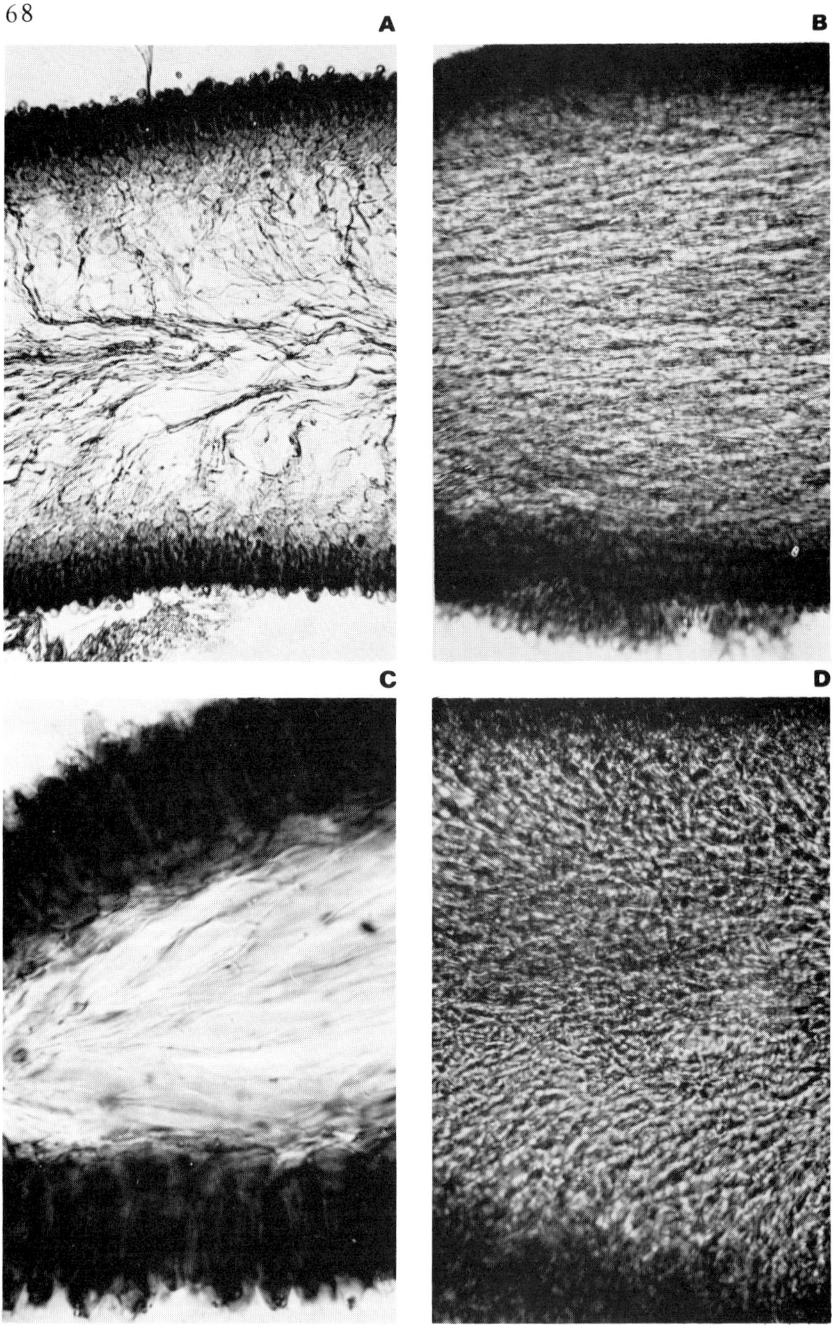

PL. X. **Hymenophoral Trama 1. A.** Divergent with obvious mediostratum and lateral strata (*Amanita muscaria*); **B.** Parallel (±) (*Tricholoma flavovirens*); **D.** Divergent; Mediostratum and Lateral Strata obscure (*Hygrophorus bakerensis*).

PL. X (PAGE 68)

C. Convergent (Pluteus cervinus)

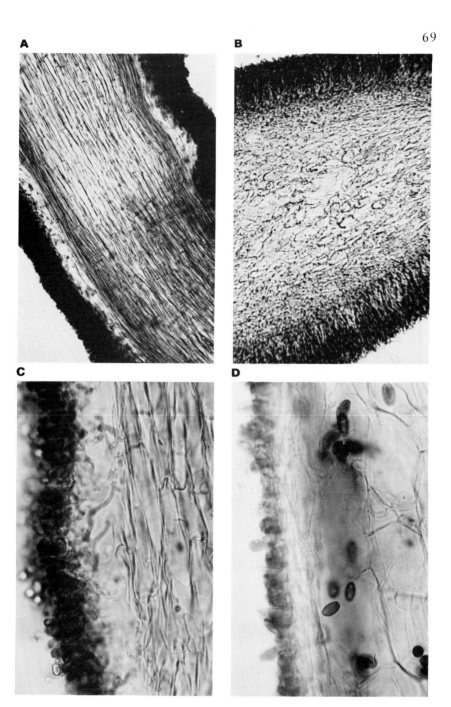

PL. XI. **Hymenophoral Trama 2.** A. Subparallel and with a gelatinized Subhymenium (*Entoloma* sp.); **B.** Interwoven (*Lentinus tortulosus*); **C.** Parallel Gill Trama composed of barrel-shaped cells; subhymenium gelatinized (*Fayodia maura*); **D.** Parallel Gill Trama; Hymenopodium composed of broad cells (*Conocybe* sp.).

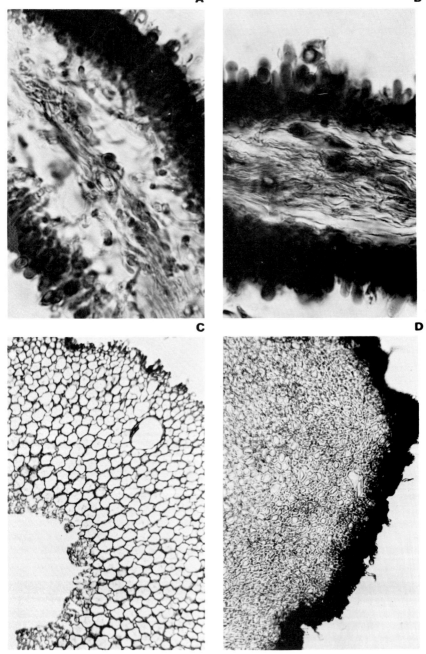

PL. XII. **Hymenophoral Trama 3. A.** Gelatinized Hymenopodium and distinct mediostratum (*Pholiota decorata*); **B.** Gelatinized Mediostratum ($\pm$) (*Paxillus involutus*); Stipe —
Transverse Section; **C.** *Coprinus* sp. **D.** *Xeromphalina cauticinalis.*

VII. CYSTIDIA

(CYSTIDIUM = SINGULAR)

Cystidia are either differentiated terminal cells of the hyphae in the hymenium which will not produce basidiospores, ie. sterile cells; or they are terminal cells of the hyphae which compose the surfaces of the basidiocarp (pelli or "cuticles") and which sometimes resemble the cystidia in the hymenium. This definition represents the one which most contemporary agaricologists utilize in their work; however it is *not* necessarily accepted by all agaricologists.

Among a myriad of possible functions cystidia are thought to: a) act as air traps and therefore maintain a favorable humidity around developing spores; b) hold adjacent gills apart, as in *Coprinus* spp. and thus assist in spore dispersal; c) aid in the evaporation of moisture and other volatile substances; and d) act as excretory organs. The fact is that the function of cystidia is as yet unknown in most instances.

Cystidia are usually morphologically distinct from basidia and typically project beyond them. Since many cystidia are a different shape than the basidia they are usually easy to differentiate. However, care should be exercised not to confuse cystidia with developing basidia, particularly those with relatively long sterigmata. A thorough survey of the hymenium should be done and all stages of basidia observed before a final decision on cystidia is made.

Cystidia which are immature, aborted, arrested in development have been called **Cystidioles**. Cystidioles are impossible to distinguish from basidioles except by nuclear analysis as in the latter there appears to be an accumulation of nuclei.

Cystidia can be classified on the basis of position (ie. topography) or on the basis of type (ie. morphology, function, or origin). Often morphologically or functionally unrelated cystidia are described on the basis of shape alone.

72

A. POSITION

Cystidia can be found on the following parts of the basidiocarp (see Fig. 22; Pl. XIII):

1) On the surfaces of the basidiocarp, excluding the hymenophoral surfaces, in which case they are called **Dermatocystidia**. (dermato = skin). Two types of dermatocystidia have been described: **Pileocystidia** (Fig. 22B,C,D; Pl. XIII B,D), cystidia found on the surface of the pileus (sometimes called pilocystidia, although we prefer to retain this term for flexuous hair-like cells), and **Caulocystidia** (Fig. 22E,F; Pl. XIII C), those found on the surface of the stipe.

2) On the surfaces of the hymenophore (therefore in the hymenium) in which case the cystidia are called **Hymenial Cystidia**. Two types of hymenial cystidia have been described: **Cheilocystidia** (Fig. 22H; Pl. XIII A), those situated on the edge of the hymenophore, and **Pleurocystidia** (Fig. 22I; Pl. XIII A), cystidia located on the sides of the hymenophore.[1]

3) In the cortex of the pileus trama, or the hymenophoral trama or the stipe trama these cystidia are called **Endocystidia** or **Tramal Cystidia**.

B. TYPE OF CYSTIDIA (MORPHOLOGY, FUNCTION, ORIGIN)

Five general types of cystidia can be recognized: **Leptocystidia, Lamprocystidia, Gloeocystidia, Hyphoids,** and **Cystidia-like Hyphae**.

I. *Leptocystidia* (Fig. 22, 23A-D, 24, 25; Pl. XVII, XVIII, XIX) are thin-walled, smooth, cystidia that do not have any distinguishable contents, are not tramal in origin, and are usually distinct from basidia. A specialized type of leptocystidia are the pavement cells of *Coprinus* which are basidiole-like in shape and are called **Brachycystidia** (Fig. 23D; Pl. XV A).

II. *Lamprocystidia* (Pl. XIV) are entirely or at least partially thick walled cystidia without distinguishable contents and are usually distinct from basidia. Five subcategories of lamprocystidia have been described; namely:

1) **Seta** (Fig. 23E) which are long, pointed lamprocystidia which turn brown to brownish black in KOH; this type of lamprocystidium is found only in a few species with a smooth hymenophore, namely *Hymenochaete* and *Phellinus* species. They are not found in agarics and boleti.

2) **Setule** (from Snell & Dick, 1957) – a skillet-shaped, pointed lamprocystidia frequently used for small setiform lamprocystidia which theoretically darkens in KOH.

3) **Setiform (Setidiform) Lamprocystidia** (Pl. XIV A) – long, pointed lamprocystidia which do not react with KOH.

---

[1] Those gill edges in which the cheilocystidia are different than the pleurocystidia or if the cheilocystidia are present and the pleurocystidia absent are called **Heteromorphous**. Two types of **Homomorphus** gill edges (those in which the hymenial elements of the gill edge are identical to those of the gill face) exist: namely, those in which cystidia are absent on the gill edge and gill face and those in which the cheilocystidia are similar to the pleurocystidia. The latter type of gill edge is called **Subheteromorphous**.

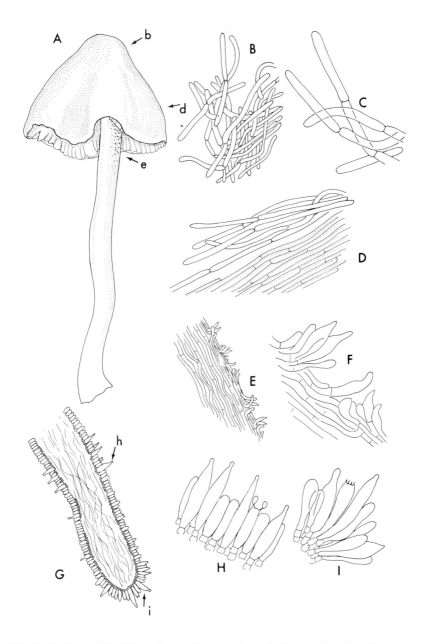

FIG. 22. **Position of Cystidia** in *Pouzarella versatilis*. **A.** Basidiocarp; **B.** Pileipellis showing pileocystidia (low magnification) taken from (b); **C.** Pileocystidia (high magnification); **D.** Pileipellis showing Pileocystidia (low magnification) taken from (d); **E.** Stipitipellis showing clusters of Caulocystidia (low magnification) taken from (e); **F.** Clusters of Caulocystidia (high magnification); **G.** Cross Section of a Gill; **H.** Pleurocystia taken from (h); **I.** Cheilocystidia taken from (i).

4) **Metuloid** (Fig. 23F, 25K; Pl. XIV B,D, Pl. XV C) – a lamprocystidium which is rounded at the apex or with a variable shaped apex. A metuloid may or may not be encrusted, pigmented, inamyloid, dextrinoid or amyloid.

5) **Mycosclerids** – lamprocystidia that are embedded in the trama (seta, setules, setiform lamprocystidia and metuloids are all either dermatocystidia or hymenial cystidia).

III. *Gloeocystidia* are versiform cystidia which stain readily with chemical reagents or have conspicuous, amorphorus or granular contents. The following categories of gloeocystidia can be distinguished –

1) **Pseudocystidia** or **Macrocystidia** (Fig. 23G; Pl. XV D) – gloeocystidia which are tramal in origin and project into and usually beyond the hymenium or the surface of the pileus or stipe. Pseudocystidia are usually metachromatic in Cresyl Blue. They also stain in the acid-aldehydes; black in sulfobenzaldehyde or red in chlorovanillin and brown in sulfoformol.

2) **Chrysocystidia** (Pl. XV B) are gloeocystidia which turn yellow or golden in aqueous alkali solutions; they are typically found in species of *Hypholoma* and *Stropharia*.

3) **Phaeocystidia** are gloeocystidia which are slighly pseudoamyloid and possess brownish contents.

4) **Coscinocystidia** are unique gloeocystidia with a sponge-like interior and sieve-like or porous surface.

IV. *Hyphoids (Hyphidia)* are versiform cystidia usually devoid of contents, thin- or thick-walled, and frequently so intricately branched so that the shape of the cystidium is complex. The following categories of hyphoids can be recognized:

1) **Asterophysis (Astrosetae)** (Fig. 23H) is a thick walled cystidium which is star-shaped at the apex and swollen below.

2) The following hyphoids are basically branched, unswollen hyphae.

   a) **Dendrophysis** (Fig. 23I) is a hyphoid with tree-like branching.

   b) **Acanthophysis** (Fig. 23J) is a hyphoid with numerous branches along its surface such that it resembles a bottle brush.

   c) **Dichophysis** (Fig. 23K; Pl. XVI A) is a hyphoid that is dichotomously branched.

V. Cystidia-like hyphae are multicellular structures which project into the hymenium. Two categories are recognized:

Cheilocatenulae (Fig. 10F; Pl. XVII B): Multicellular hyphae with differentiated elements which often disarticulate. These form "cystidia" on the gill edge of certain agarics (eg. species of *Agaricus, Armillaria mellea, Amanita* and *Phylloporus*).

Cystidioid Hyphae (Fig. 8F, 11F): Similar to cheilocatenulae except the elements are undifferentiated.

C. SHAPES OF CYSTIDIA

Cystidia take three basic shapes; 1) those with essentially parallel sides in which the width remains the same along the entire length of the cell. Relatively narrow, thread-like cystidia are called **Filiform** (Fig. 24A). Filiform cystidia are

75

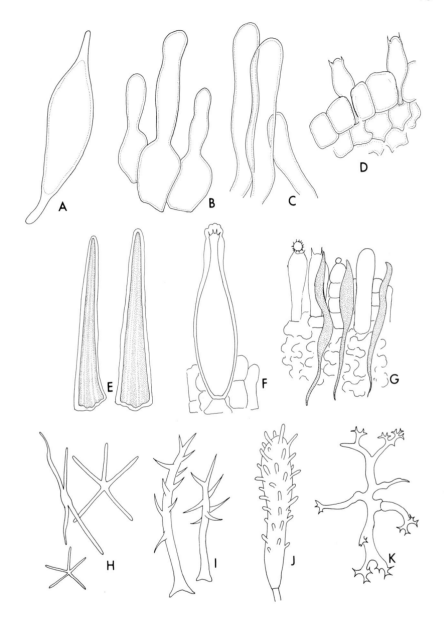

FIG. 23. **Types and Shapes of Cystidia. A.** Ventricose-Rostrate Leptocystidia (*Leptonia convexa*); **B.** Ventricose-Rostrate Leptocystidia (*Leptonia exalbida*); **C.** Clavate Leptocystidia (*Leptonia vinaceobrunnea*); **D.** Brachycystidia (*Coprinus* sp.); **E.** Aculeate Seta (*Hymenochaete* sp.); **F.** Obclavate Metuloid (*Inocybe decipiens*); **G.** Pseudocystidia (*Lactarius fuliginosus*); **H.** Asterophysis (*Asterostroma* sp.) **I.** Dendrophysis (*Dendrochaete* sp.); **J.** Acanthophysis; **K.** Dichophysis (*Vararia* sp.).

frequently not recorded as cystidia but as hyphal projections, eg. in *Hygrophorus laetus*, while cystidia which are broader than filiform cells are called **Cylindrical** (Fig. 24B). 2) Those in which the apex is thicker or broader than above middle. These cystidia taper from the middle to the base. 3) Those which are broadest in the middle and which taper toward the base and the apex; these cystidia are called **Ventricose** (Fig. 23A-B, 24C, 25J). If the cystidium is only somewhat thickened at the middle, it is called **Subventricose**.

1. Apex

A number of terms describe the apex of a cystidium which may be **Obtuse** (rounded), **Acute** (sharp pointed), or **Elongate**. The apex can be in the shape of a head or a ball (a **Caput**), a beak or prolonged extension (a **Rostrum**), or a single pointed extension (a **Mucro**). If more than one protuberance occurs, they are called **Appendages**.

Obtuse Apices: Several terms, outlined below, have been used to describe cystidia in which the apex is obtuse and not elongate; most of these cystidia are also swollen at the apical end and tapered toward the middle or the base; in some, however, the middle or base can be swollen and the apex tapered.

Claviform: cystidia which are basically narrow except for the swollen apex which scarcely suggests a minute club.

Cylindro-Clavate (Fig. 24D; Pl.XVII D): cystidia which are basically cylindrical yet the swollen apex gives it the shape of a small club.

Clavate (Fig. 23C, 24E; Pl. XVIII C): cystidia in which the apical portion is enlarged so that it appears decidedly club-shaped (like a baseball bat).

In a sense, the types of cystidium described above are gradually tapered with the smallest diameter occurring at the middle or basal portion of the cystidium (see the diagram).

Several terms have been used to describe cystidia in which the taper is abrupt and the apical portion is quite swollen.

Sphaeropedunculate (Fig. 24F; Pl. XVII A): a cystidium in which the apical portion is swollen into a spherical (sphaero- or sphero-) tip and tapers abruptly near the middle to an elongated basal peg or peduncle.

Napiform (Fig. 24G): a cystidium which is swollen or bulbous above but tapers rather abruptly to the base, like a turnip (*napus*); therefore, turnip-shaped.

Turbinate (Fig. 24H): a cystidium which is swollen at the apex and the taper begins near the middle and becomes quite abrupt at the base, like a top; therefore top-shaped.

Vesiculate (vesiculose, vesicular) (Fig. 24I): a cystidium in which the entire cell is inflated like a large sac or bladder (vesicle). Only the very base is abruptly tapered; therefore, vesicle-shaped.

In some cystidia with obtuse apices the cell is tapered toward the apex. If the cystidium is slightly swollen at the base like a club and gradually tapers toward the apex, it is called **Obclavate** (Fig. 25E) which means reversely (ob-) clavate. If the cystidium is ventricose or subventricose at the base and the apex more or less abruptly tapered into a relatively broad extension, it is called **Pyriform** (Fig. 24J) (pear-shaped) or **Ampulliform** (**Ampullate** if flask-shaped). Pyriform and

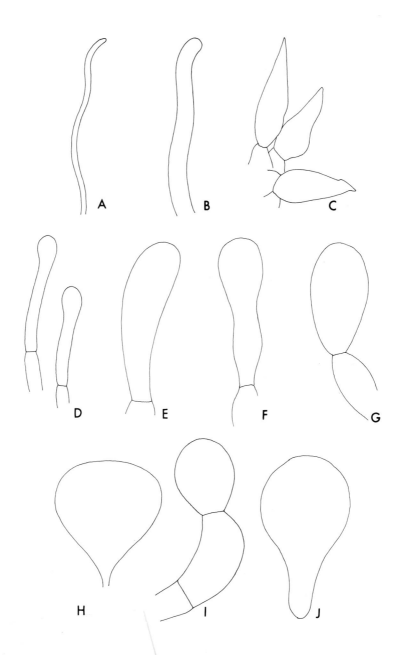

orm; **B.** Cylindrical (*Leptonia trichomata*); **C.** Ventricose
umis); **D.** Cylindro-Clavate (*Entoloma sericatum*); **E.**
e; **I.** Vesiculate (*Leptonis fulva*); **J.** Pyriform.

ampulliform cystidia are also considered under cystidia with extended apices.

Acute Apices: The following terms apply to those cystidia in which the immediate apex is pointed (acute) and not elongate.

Aciculate (acicular) (Fig. 25A): the cystidium is filiform with an acute apex, like a needle; therefore needle-shaped.

Aculeate (trichiform) (Fig. 23E, 25B): the cystidium is tapered so that only the very basal portion is relatively swollen. The entire cystidium is slender and shaped like a spine; therefore, spine-shaped.

Subulate (Fig. 25C): a cystidium which is swollen between the middle and the slightly tapered base, like an awl (subula = awl); therefore awl-shaped.

Lanceolate (Fig. 25D): a cystidium which is subventricose to slightly swollen at or near the middle and is tapered at both ends, like a lance; therefore, lance-shaped.

Two terms refer to degrees of abruptness of an acute apex. If the taper is gradual the cystidium is called **Acuminate** (Fig. 24C) and if the apex is extended into a single, abrupt point it is called **Mucronate** (Fig. 25F). The latter term is meant to emphasize the extension; therefore this word will also be found in the next set of terms applicable to cystidial apices.

Apices with protuberances: In those cystidia with protuberant apices, the extension may be in the shape of a ball, a beak or a sharp point.

Caput (ball or head-like protuberances): cystidia with a head are called **Capitate**.

Capitulate (Fig. 25G; Pl. XIX A): cystidia which are basically filiform or cylindrical except for the apex which is swollen into a small knob or head.

Tibiiform (Fig 25H; Pl. XVIII B, XIX B): cystidia which are basically subventricose with a long and narrow neck and the apex swollen into a head or knob, like the tibia bone.

Lecythiform (Fig. 25I; Pl. XVIII D): cystidia which are ventricose with the middle tapered into a narrow neck and the apex swollen into a head, like a bowling pin (lecythiform refers to a Greek stoppered bottle). These cystidia are characteristically symmetrical.

Utriform: cystidia which have a slight constriction below a large, round head, like a bladder; therefore bladder-shaped.

Rostrum (beak-like or finger-like protuberances): cystidia with some type of beak-like protuberance are called **Rostrate**.

Ventricose-Rostrate (Fig. 23A-B; Pl. SVIII C, XIX B): cystidia in which the basal and middle portions are ventricose and the apex is extended into a beak-like protrusion.

Lageniform (Cucurbitiform, Sicyoid) (Pl. XVIII A, XIX B): cystidia in which the base is swollen and the middle and apical portion is tapered into a long beak, like a gourd; therefore, gourd-shaped.

Ampulliform: similar to ventricose-rostrate except the rostrum is quite broad, like a flask; therefore flask-shaped.

Pyriform (Fig. 24J): like ampulliform except the cystidium appears more rounded, like a pear; therefore pear-shaped.

Obclavate (Fig. 25E): a cystidium which is swollen like a club at the base and gradually narrows at the middle and apex; reversely clavate.

Mucro (one protuberance): cystidia in which the apex narrows abruptly into

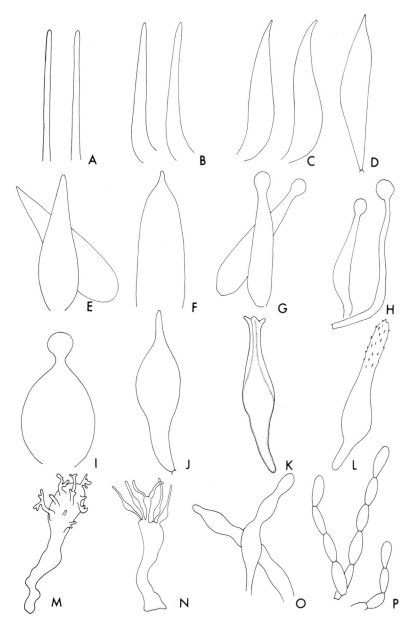

FIG. 25. **Cystidia Shape II. A.** Aciculate; **B.** Aculeate (*Pouzarella nodospora*); **C.** Subulate (*Mycena atkinsoniana*); **D.** Lanceolate (*Mycena corticaticeps*); **E.** Obclavate (*Mycena sub-*

a pointed protuberance are called **Mucronate**.

Appendages (more than one protuberance in which case the extensions are called appendages): often these cystidia are called forked or **Furcate**.

Digitate (Fig. 25J): a cystidium with two to several finger-like, apical protuberances; the remaining portion of the cell is usually swollen.

Cornuate (Barbellate) (Fig. 25K; Pl. XVC): a cystidium with the apical appendages in the shape of horns.

Echinate (Fig. 25L): Cystidia which have numerous spine-like protuberances over the entire surface or limited to the apical portion.

Diverticulate (Fig. 25M; Pl. XVI D): cystidia which have numerous peg-like protuberances located either over the apical portion or over the entire surface.

Broom Cells (Fig. 25N; Pl. XVI B): cystidia which have at the apex several pointed protuberances which are not horn-like and are typically dark in color; the remaining portion of the cystidium is swollen.

Cystide en Brosse: A general term used widely in all languages for cystidia here defined as diverticulate and echinate.

In many instances the cystidia on any one surface assume so many shapes that it is difficult to describe all of the variations. These cystidia are called **Versiform** which means variable in shape. Furthermore cystidia may have flexuous or sinuous (wavy) walls as if the cystidia has alternately contracted and expanded. If the contractions and expansions are irregular the cystidium is called **Strangulated** (Fig. 25O; Pl. XIX D); if they are regular so that the cell appears as if made of beads, the cystidium is called **Moniliform** (or **Torulose**) (Fig. 25P; Pl. VIII D).

D. PIGMENTATION AND INCRUSTATIONS

When cystidia which have vacuolar or cytoplasmic pigments are observed mass the gill edges appear colored. The macroscopic term for colored gill edges is marginate. Pigmented cystidia should be observed in water since the pigment is often soluble in an aqueous, alkali solution. Cystidia may also have membranal or intercellular pigments which should be studied as indicated in the section on pigmentation of hyphae.

Cystidia can also be ornamented, particularly at the apex or middle portions. Cystidia with a crystalline or amorphous deposit are called **Incrusted (Encrusted)** (P. XIX C). The chemistry and function of such incrustations are as yet unknown.

E. CHEMICAL REACTIONS

Several chemicals are used in studying cystidia. These are *Melzer's* reagent in which the cystidia may turn blue-black (*amyloid*); reddish brown (*dextrinoid*), or remain hyaline (*inamyloid*). Cystidia stained in cresy blue turn the contents blue and are called **Metachromatic**. In **Acid-Aldehydes** (sulfobenzaldehyde, etc.) cystidia turn either blue, black or green. Because these chemicals stain the cystidia distinctive colors, one can observe the internal contents and also trace the elements back into the trama. The KOH-Phloxine-Congo Red mounts help distinguish cystidia from surrounding cells and from the trama proper.

F. REFERENCES

Cystidia have been thoroughly defined and outlined by numerous investigators. If the reader wishes to review the various viewpoints concerning cystidia the following articles should be studied: Locquin (1953), Romagnesi (1944), Lohwag (1941), Buller (1924), Bas (1969), Smith (1966), Lentz (1954) and Singer (1975). The above presentation on cystidia represents a concensus of the authors' opinions with the main objective being to aid an individual in describing mushrooms or to arrive at an understanding of terms used in technical descriptions and mycological literature.

82

A

B

C

D

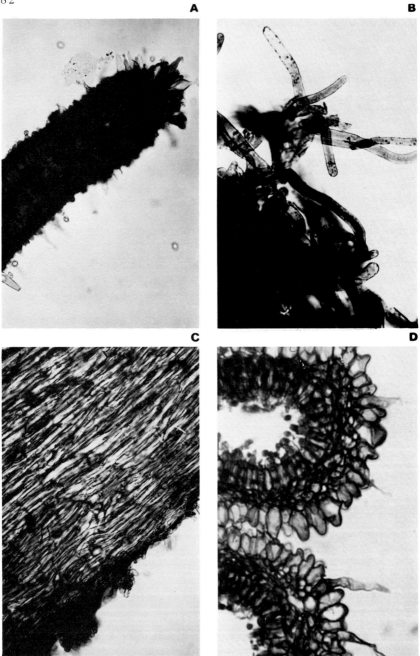

PL. XIII. **Cystidia: Position A.** Cheilocystidia (top right) and Pleurocystidia (both sides) (*Pouzarella versatilis*); **B.** Pileocystidia (*Pouzarella versatilis*); **C.** Clusters of Caulocystidia (*Pouzarella versatilis*); **D.** Pileocystidia (*Coprinus*, prepared slide).

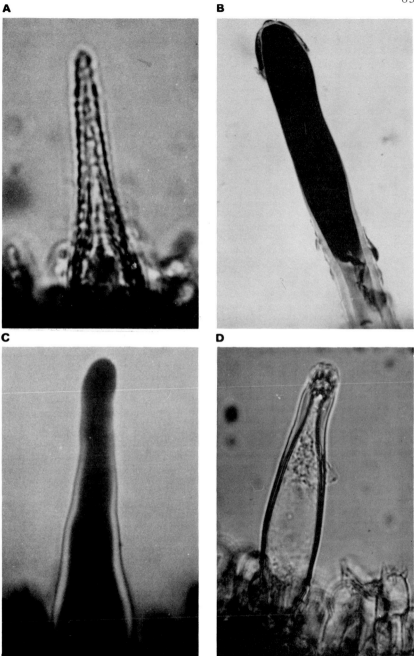

PI. XIV Lamprocystidia A. Setiform Lamprocystidia (*Hohenbuehlia niger*); B. Metuloid (*Chroogomphus tomentosus*); C. Lamprocystidia with variable wall thichkness (*Pholiota velagelatinosa*); D. Metuloid (*Inocybe decipiens*).

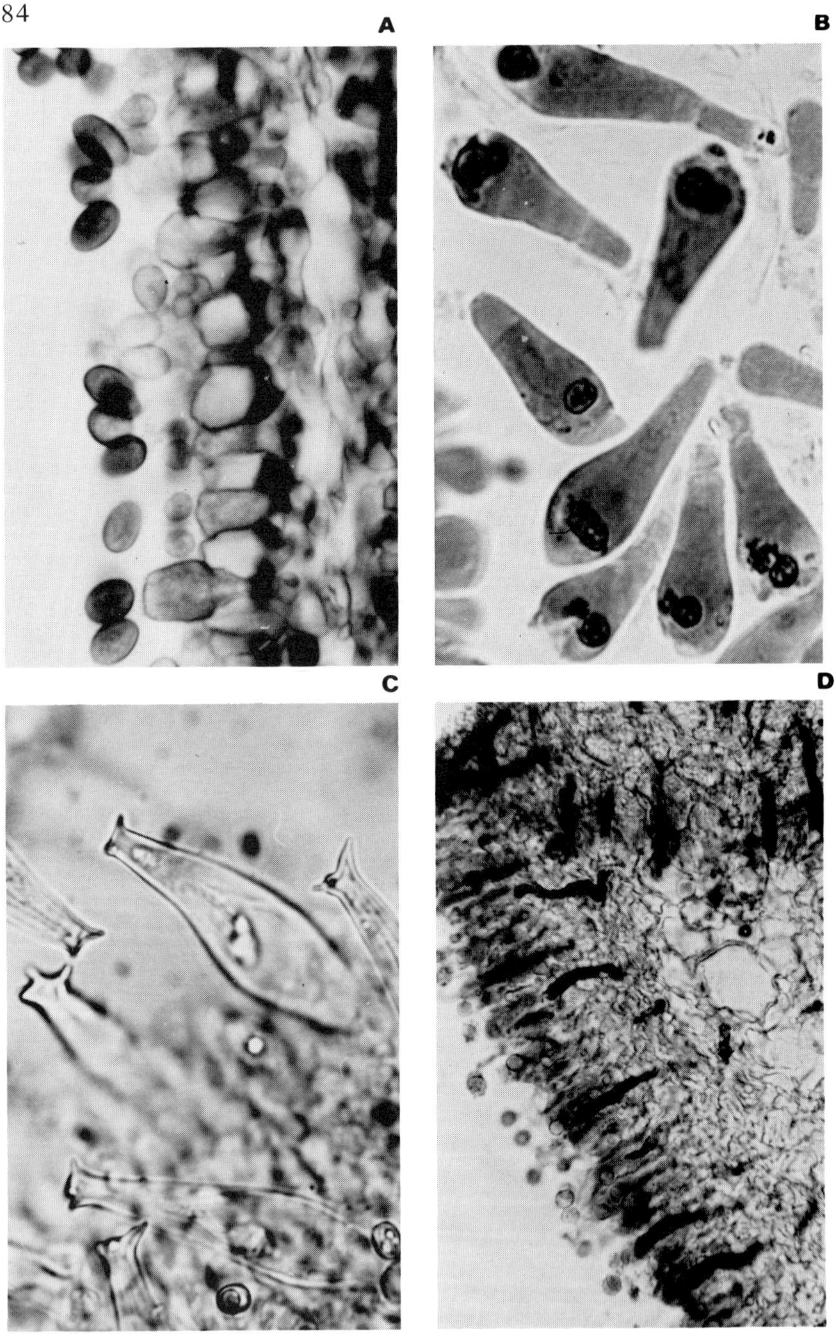

PL. XV. **Cystidia 1. A.** Pavement Cells (between basidia) (*Coprinus* sp.); **B.** Chrysocystidia (*Stropharia hornemanii*); **C.** Cornuate Metuloids (*Pluteus cervinus*); **D.** Macrocystidia (dark staining) (*Lactarius fuliginosus*).

A

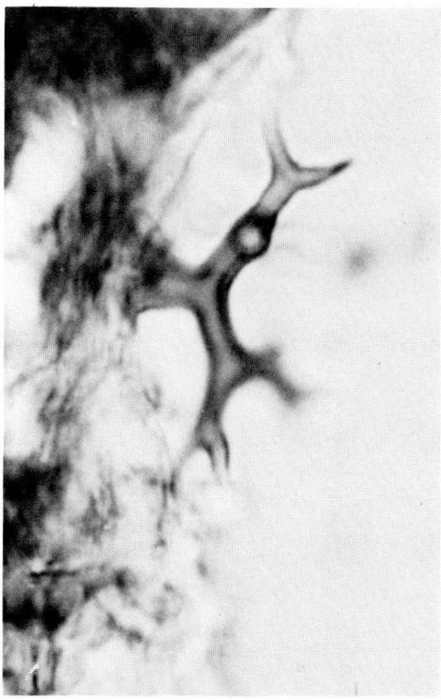

B

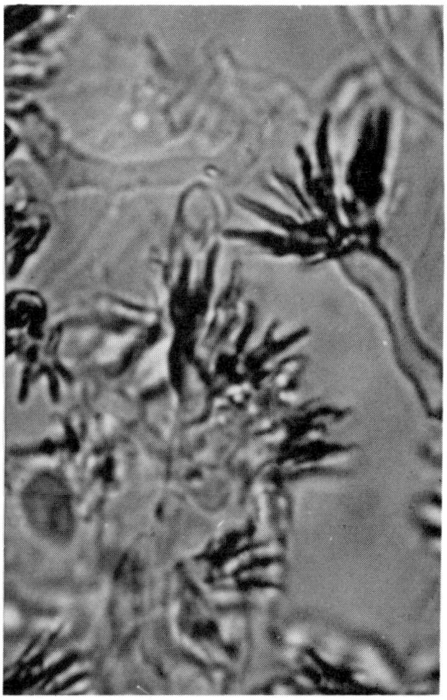

C

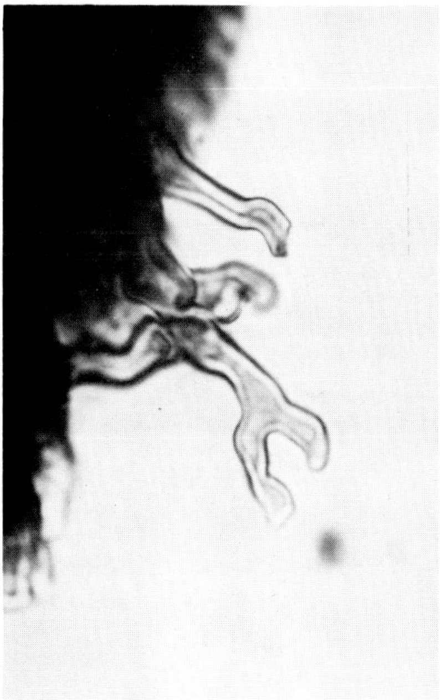

D

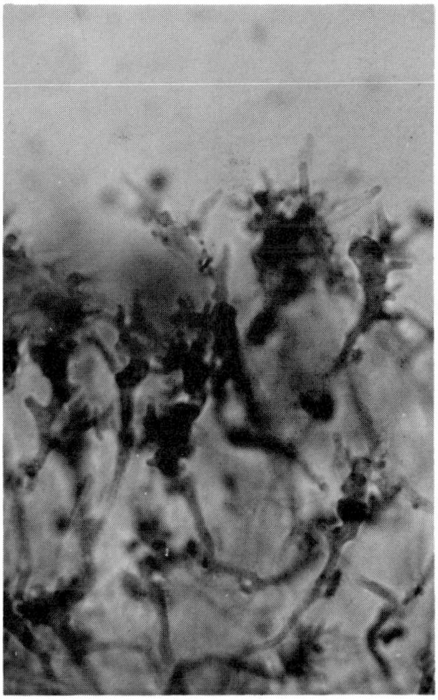

PL. XVI. **Cystidia 2. A.** Dichophysis (*Vararia* sp.); **B.** Broom Cells (*Marasmius plicatilis*); **C.** Horn-shaped Caulocystidia (*Xeromphalina cauticinalis*); **D.** Diverticulate Cheilocystidia (*Mycena epipterygia*).

86

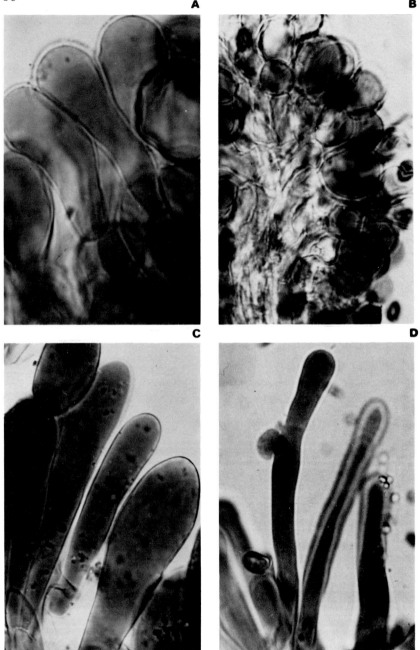

PL. XVII. **Cystidia 3. A.** Sphaeropedunculate (±) pileocystidia (Leptocystidia) (*Leptonia lividocyanula*); **B.** Cheilocatenulae (*Agaricus sylvaticus*); **C.** Clavate Pileocystidia (Leptocystidia) (*Leptonia gracilipes*); **D.** Cylindro-clavate Cheilocystidia (Leptocystidia) (*Psathyrella rigidipes*).

87

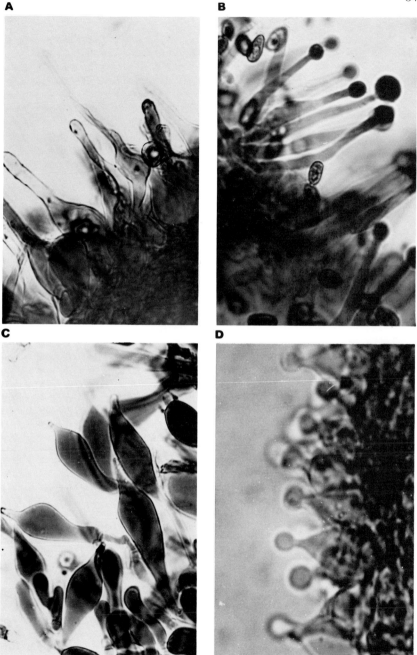

PL. XVIII. Cheilocystidia and Leptocystidia Shape A. Lageniform (*Nolanea* sp.); B. Tibiiform (*Galerina tibiicystis*); C. Ventricose-Rostrate (*Leptonia perfusca*); D. Lecythyform (*Conocybe megalospora*).

88

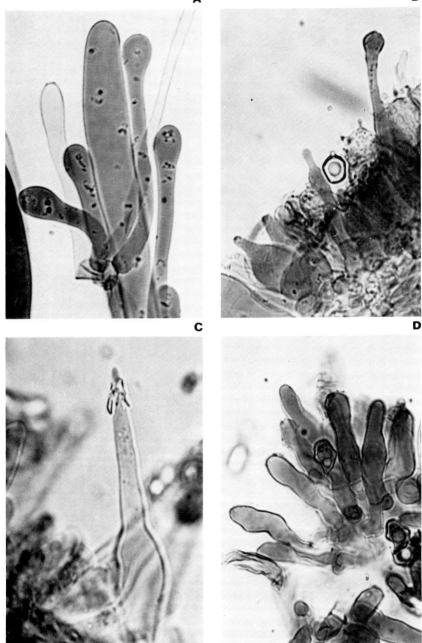

PL. XIX. **Cystidia 4. A.** Capitulate Pileocystidia (Leptocystidia) (*Leptonia vinaceobrunnea*);
B. Ventricose-Rostrate (lower left), Lageniform (middle), Tibiiform (±), Cheilocystidia
(Leptocystidia) (*Leptonia pseudobulbipes*); **C.** Encrusted, Fusoid-Ventricose Cheilocystidium with Acute apex (Leptocystidia) (*Melanoleuca grammopodium*); **D.** Strangulated Cheilocystidia (Leptocystidia) (*Nolanea hirtipes*).

VIII. BASIDIUM AND BASIDIOLE

A. BASIDIA

In agarics and boletes the basidium is typically single-celled and thin-walled. Normally it bears four spores and is clavate to broadly clavate when mature and fusoid to narrowly clavate when young. Such a basidium is called a **Holobasidium** (Pl. XX, XXI) in contrast to the **Heterobasidium** of rusts and jelly fungi which is either shaped differently or multicellular (see the diagrams).

The holobasidium of agarics and boletes bears the basidiospores on sickle-shaped apical extensions called **Sterigma** (Fig. 27E; Pl. XX, XXI) (sterigmata = plural). The basidiospores are slightly offset on each of the sterigmata so that they are attached obliquely with respect to the longitudinal axis of the basidia. This type of spore attachment is called **Heterotropic** (Fig. 28A; Pl. XX D) in contrast to the **Orthotropic** (Fig. 28B) spore attachment of the puff-balls and their allies (ie. true Gasteromycetes) and some rather specialized species of *Hiatulopsis*. In an orthotropic spore attachment the basidiospores are situated symmetrically about the basidium and their longitudinal axis corresponds to the longitudinal axis of the basidia. Not all Gasteromycetes have orthotropic spore attachment and many of those that do not would appear to be related to agarics with heterotropic attachment.

A holobasidium typically possesses a single, diploid nucleus which, as the basidium matures, undergoes meiosis and produces 4, haploid nuclei. In all agarics and boletes the spindles of the second meiotic division are horizontal or subhorizontal; such a basidium is called a **Chiastobasidium**. The contrasting basidium is a **Stichobasidium** in which the spindles of the second meiotic division are vertically situated and parallel to the longitudinal axis of the basidium. Stichobasidia are typical of the agaric-like *Cantharellus* and *Gomphus* and are also found in some basidiocarps with a non-gilled hymenophore.

After meiosis the haploid nuclei are pushed towards the apex of the basidium and out through the sterigma due to increased pressure created by an enlarging vacuole. The pressure increases until the spores are forcibly ejected from the basidium. Forceful spore discharge is associated with holobasidia that have hetertropic spore attachment. The nuclei typically migrate into one sterigma at a time. Therefore depending on the maturity of the basidium, 1 to 4 basidiospores are visible. Care should be taken to observe the appearance of the basidium during different stages of spore maturation since immature basidia (look for signs of developing sterigmata) can be confused with hymenial cystidia. The stage of maturity should be considered when counting the number of spores per basidium.

The basidia usually mature in an apparent haphazard fashion in the hymenium so that an approximate equal number of basidia are mature at one time; such a type of hymenium is called **Aequihymeniiferous**. In mushrooms with an aequihymeniiferous hymenium, the gill faces are not exactly parallel to one another and the gill trama is thicker near the pileus context than near the gill edge; therefore the gills are constructed like a knife blade and in cross section the gill is wedge-shaped. In *Panaeolus*, although aequihymeniiferous, the basidia ripen in patches giving a spotted appearance to the mature gill.

In the genus *Coprinus*, however, the gill faces are parallel to one another and the gill trama is more or less uniformly thickened from near the gill edge to the area near the pileus context. The basidia in this type of hymenium mature from the gill edge upward and, after the maturation of basidia and the discharge of the basidiospores, the area of hymenium which produced the spores begins to autodeliquesce eventually turning the gills to an ink-like fluid. This type of hymenium found in *Coprinus* is called **Inaequihymeniiferous** (Pl. XX A).

The holobasidia typical of agarics and boletes vary in shape, size, wall thickness and number of spores per basidium. They are outlined below.

Spore number: The typical number of spores on a holobasidium is four, however several species have been described which possess only two-spores per basidium. The two--spored basidia produce spores which are proportionately larger than spores from typical four-spored basidia. Single spored basidia, rare in mushrooms and boleti, are more fusoid in shape than the clavate 2-4-spored basidia. Although uncommon, a few species of agarics are characterized by 3-spored basidia as in *Coprinus trisporus* which also has a few 4-spored basidia. In *Cantharellus*, some basidia are 6-8-spored.

Shape and size: Most basidia of the agarics and boletes are clavate to broadly clavate and roughly 2-4 times longer than wide. However, the basidia of *Hygrophorus* and its segregate genera are cylindro-clavate and 5-8 times longer than wide; consequently the gills appear thick and waxy. Care should be taken since not all thick and waxy gills are due to long basidia. For example, the waxy gills of *Laccaria* are caused by a thick gill trama. Furthermore, there are several instances of long basidia in the agarics (e.g. in *Catathelasma* and some *Mycena* species) which do not create thick, waxy gills.

Some basidia are quite small and/or squat. Typical examples can be found in *Agaricus* (small), *Conocybe* (short), several species of *Psathyrella* (short) and *Russula* (globose). In *Coprinus* the basidia may be of 1, 2, or 3 different and distinct sizes thus allowing maturation of an entire gill section simultaneously. Dimorphism is also found in *Hygrophorus militaris*.

Wall: The wall of a typical holobasidium is usually very thin and observed only as a line in the compound microscope. In contrast, in a few agarics the basidium is thick-walled (0.5 μm thick or thicker). Such a basidium is called a **Sclerobasidium**. Sclerobasidia are usually, but not always, sterile. An example of sterile sclerobasidia can be found in some species of *Hygrotrama* whereas fertile sclerobasidia can be found in some species of *Fayodia*.

B. BASIDIOLES

Basidioles are considered immature, aborted or developmental stages of basidia. Basidioles are usually clavate to broadly clavate and therefore similar in shape to basidia; basidioles, as do basidia, typically originate from the subhymenium.

Some hymenial elements, particularly in the genus *Coprinus*, are similar to basidioles in structure although slightly more differentiated; they differ mainly from basidioles because they are larger and more inflated. They have been called **Brachybasidioles** (Fig. 23D; Pl. XV A; Pl. XX A) (or **Brachycystidia, Pseudoparaphyses, Coprinoid Appendages** and **Pavement Cells**). These brachybasidioles overlap to form a pavement through which basidia project. They apparently act as spacing agents. The type of hymenium typified by this construction has been called a **Coprinoid Hymenial Structure**.

In this section mention should be made of **Hyphal Pegs**. In the extreme form they consist of thick-walled more or less interwoven hymenial hyphae pushing up between the basidia. Less typically a single, very narrow, thick-walled, sub-acute hypha constitutes the peg.

C. CHEMICAL REACTIONS

Basidia usually do not react with most reagents. Three exceptions are the **Cyanophilous** reaction of basidia with Cotton Blue, the **Metachromatic** reaction with Cresyl Blue and the **Carminophilous** (Pl. XXI C) reaction with acetocarmine. Examples of these reactions are found in the study lists at the end of this book. In a KOH – phloxine – congo red mount, the cytoplasm of basidia stains an even pink which is typical of hyaline thin-walled basidia.

92

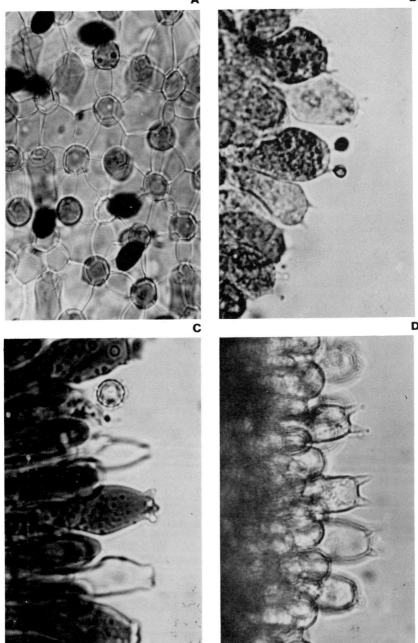

PL. XX. **Inaequihymeniiferous Hymenium and Holobasidia. A.** Inaequihymeniiferous
Hymenium (sufrace view) showing basidia (dark cells), pavement cells (light cells) and spores
(black) (*Coprinus niveus*); Holobasidia; **B.** *Nolanea* sp.; **C.** *Lactarius fuliginosus*; **D.** *Inocybe
decipiens*.

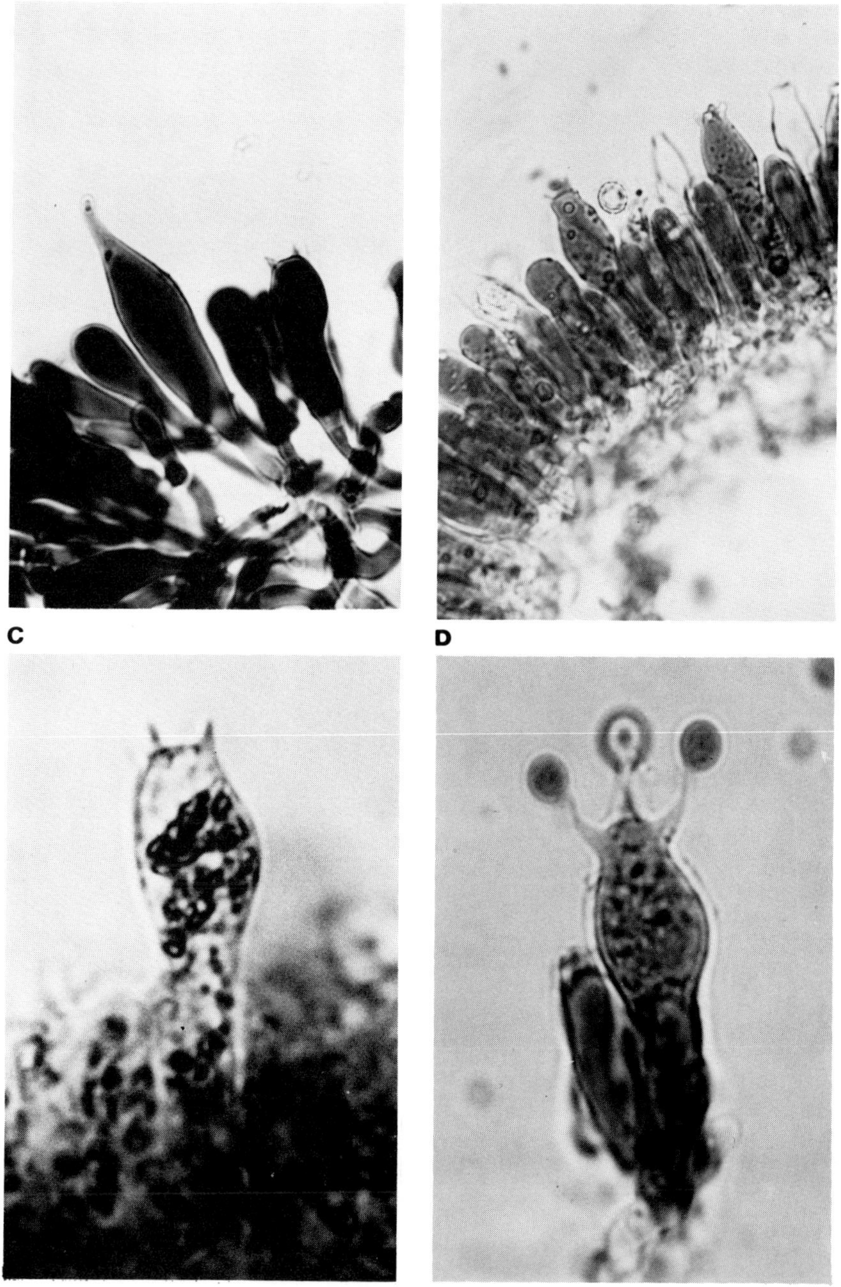

PL. XXI. **Hymenium and Basidia A.** Holobasidia and Ventricose-Rostrate Cheilocystidium of *Leptonia perfusca*; B. Hymenium of *Lactarius fuliginosus* (note basidia in various stages of development); C. Carminophilous Holobasidium (*Lyophyllum multiceps*); D. Holobasidium with Heterotrophically attached basidiospores (*Lactarius fuliginosus*).

IX. BASIDIOSPORES

The use of spores as a taxonomic character has been widely accepted since the very inception of agaricology. By 1821, Elias Fries, as well as many of his predecessors, emphasized spore print color. Since that time and concommitant with the development of improved optic systems emphasis has been placed on spore shape, size, symmetry, and ornamentation. Recently the different layers of the spore wall have been emphasized through the use of the electron microscope (for example, see Pegler and Young's study on the spore, 1971 and 1977). Consequently if the study of the microscopic features of agarics and boletes is to be mastered, a fundamental knowledge of basidiospores is certainly a requirement.

A. HOW TO STUDY BASIDIOSPORES

In order to study basidiospores from freshly collected fruiting bodies, it is best to work from a spore print since you will need to use mature, discharged spores. Spore prints can be obtained in a number of ways. It is convenient to carry small pieces of white paper, microscope slides and small boxes or various sized tins (sucret boxes, snuff boxes, etc.) in your collecting basket. Cut the stipe from one basidiocarp of your collection just below the attachment of the gills. Place the pileus with the gills resting on a piece of white paper and/or a microscope slide. The latter works best for small basidiocarps. After this, either wrap the pileus and paper (slide) in waxed paper (*do not use baggies or similar plastic material*) and place the wrapped container safely in your basket *or* place the pileus and paper (glass slide) in a tin or box and pack securely with moist moss or leaves. If time is not available for these procedures while collecting, the same procedures should be followed upon return to the laboratory. If a spore print cannot be obtained, see if spores are available in a mass on some portion of the basidiocarp, eg. the ring, near the apex of the stipe or among the cortina fibrils. If no spores are available, the only other sources of study material are from spores washed from a small segment of gill by agitation in a drop of water on a slide or from spores present in the radial or tangential section of the pileus or gills. Spores frequently are abundant in the slides of a single gill used to study the gross features of the cheilocystidia or in the sections of gills used to study the shape and size of the ancillary structures (cheilocystidia and pleurocystidia) in the hymenium. The same locations are to be utilized when studying spores from dried material; however, many more spores should be studied from dried specimens than from fresh ones since some spores usually shrink or change shape when undergoing drying and the whole range from mature to immature and from normal to abnormal may be encountered.

First study some of the spores in water by *either* scraping the spores from the spore print *or* placing the gill or sections of the gills in a drop of water on a microscope slide. Several precautions must be taken at this time: 1) Use a minimal amount of water; spores are small cells and will float out from under a cover slip if too much liquid is used; 2) remove all debris from the liquid with your needles while viewing with a dissecting scope or good hand lens; any piece of dirt or dust will raise the cover slip enough to hinder studying the features of the spore and may crack it when racking the stage up and down; 3) Use #1 cover slips (size 22x30 mm) if possible. Most spores must be studied using the oil lens of a compound microscope. A thicker cover slip (size 2,3) will raise the height of the material sufficiently so that pressure from the oil lens will more easily break the cover slip; 4) If spores have to be studied from gill sections, the sections must be thin enough to study the material under oil.

Water should routinely be the first liquid in which spores are studied since color as well as ornamentation of many spores are affected by more caustic substances. After water is used, spores should be studied in several, different liquids (see P. 21).

Note the following features when studying spores with a compound microscope: spore color, attachment, symmetry, contents and construction of the wall as well as size, ornamentation and shape.

B. SPORE FEATURES

1. Spore Color

With practice, the color of spores can be determined even under a microscope. If the pigment is at all pronounced, it can usually be determined from spores which are observed in water. The spore color is easily seen in a spore print because the spores are collected *en masse*. (For example, light yellow spores in a spore print may appear hyaline when viewed in water under a microscope.) As more microscopic proficiency in studying spores is achieved, spore color can be judged with a fair degree of accuracy from spores in aqueous alkaline solutions. Remember, spores in these liquids are generally one or two shades lighter than in a spore print.

Finally, spore color should be studied immediately when placed in any liquid since many spores change color, some right away, others only after a time. For example, the spore color of *Bolbitius* spores are rich golden yellow in water but become light rust brown with time; in alkaline solutions they become dark rust brown.

2. Spore Attachment

Before any feature of spores can be understood, it is absolutely necessary to understand how a spore is attached to a basidium. A thorough understanding of spore attachment will provide the background to understand spore terminology as applied to shape and topography.

Figure 26A shows three spores which are still attached to the sterigmata of the basidium. Spores 1 & 3 appear in **Side-View** (or **Profile** or **Dorsiventral**). The fourth spore (#4) has already been released. A view of the top of the basidium (Fig. 26B) demonstrates the relationship of the spores to each other. The different views can have different shapes and hence different measurements. The example shown in the figure shows the **Face-View** (#2) in which the spore can be separated longitudinally into two halves which are mirror images of one another. However, a similar line drawn through a spore viewed in **Side** view may or may not divide the spore into mirror images. If it does not, the spore is said to be **Inequilateral**.

In side view, the spore has a concave side which faces the imaginary axis of the basidium; this side is called **Adaxial** (ad = towards; axial = axis; therefore the side towards the axis) or the **Dorsal** side. The convex side of the spore which faces away or outward from the imaginary axis of the basidium is called the **Abaxial** (ab = away; axial = axis) or **Ventral** side. In an asymmetrical spore as diagrammed in the figure, the dorsal side is concave (side view) whereas the fat or pot-bellied portion of the spore is always on the ventral side of the spore. (Note – many tummies are pot-bellied and tummies are on the opposite side (ventral) to the back or dorsum.) Fortunately, the face view of a spore, whether looking at dorsal or ventral surfaces, will yield similar length and width measurements. Consequently the distinction between the dorsal and ventral faces of a spore is not emphasized.

The top of the spore as it sits on the basidium is called the **Apex** or the **Distal End** (Fig. 27A). Any feature describing this end of the spore is usually modified by the adjective, **Apical**; for example, an **Apical Pore** (Fig. 27B). The bottom of a spore as it sits on the basidium is called the **Base** or **Proximal End** (Fig. 27C) of the spore.

The point of attachment of the spore on the sterigma of the basidium is best called the **Hilar Appendix** or **Appendage** (Fig. 27D; Pl. XXXIII B, XXIV C). Thus some agaricologists avoid the use of the term apiculus which can be misleading since it is found at the base of the spore and not at the apex; the term apiculus is of Latin derivation referring to an apex, (ie. the apex of the sterigmata). Pegler and Young (1971) have demonstrated that there are two distinctly different types of hilar appendages and of hila (plural for hilum) in the agarics; these are called the **Nodulose** and **Open-pore** types. The nodulose hilum,

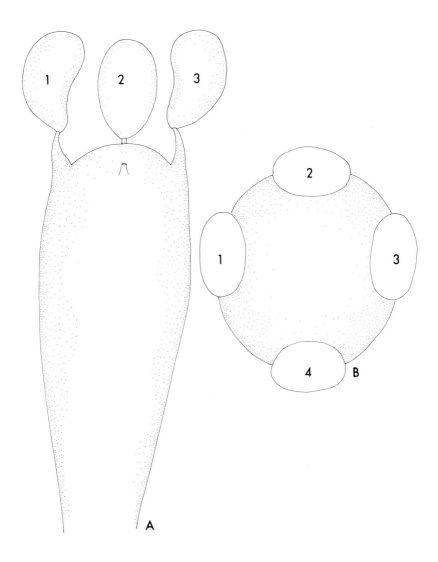

FIG. 26. **Spore Attachment. A.** View of entire basidium with three basidiosproes attached. Spores 1 and 3 are seen in Side View; Spore 2 is seen in Face View. **B.** Top view of Basidium with all four spores attached.

98

possessed by many species with hyaline spores, consists of an approximately circular area which is completely sealed and which is outlined by several, tiny, roundish bumps. In the open-pore type, possessed by species with colored spores, the hilum is a depression which is not nodulose and which exists as a break in the wall of the hilar appendix. Opposite the hilum, on the appendage, there is a pore or tear in the wall. These features are best seen with the aid of the electron microscope since the hilar appendix often appears hyaline and strongly refractive under the light microscope.

In face view an applanation or flattening of the spore wall creates a distinctive area on the dorsal side of the spore near the hilar appendix. This depression is called the **Suprahilar Disc** or more commonly, a **Plage**. If the plage is amyloid it is called the **Hilar Spot**, ie. an amyloid suprahilar plage, as in some *Russula* spp.

In all basidiocarps of fleshy fungi which forcefully eject the basidiospores and from which spore prints can be obtained, the spores are attached obliquely to the sterigma; this type of spore attachment is called **Heterotropic** (Fig. 28A; Pl. XXI D). In heterotropic spore attachment, the longitudinal axis of the sterigma

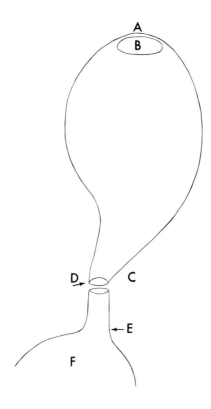

FIG. 27. **Parts of a Spore. A.** Apex or Distal end; **B.** Apical (Germ) Pore; **C.** Base or Proximal end; **D.** Apiculus (Hilar Appendage); **E.** Sterigma; **F.** Basidium.

99

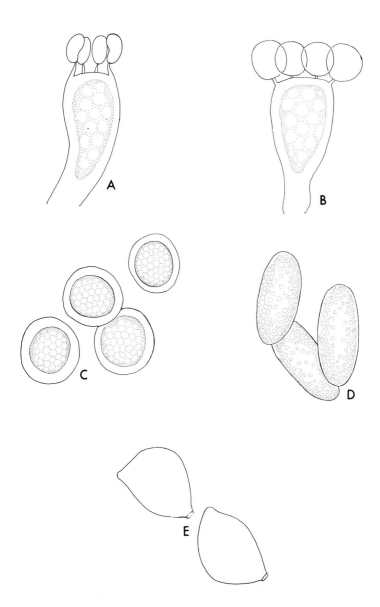

FIG. 28. **Spore Attachment and Symmetry. A,** Heterotrophic Spore attachment *(Mycena pura)*; **B.** Orthotropic Spore Attachment *(Lycoperdon* sp.); **C.** Radially Symmetrical Spores *(Cyathus lesueurii)*; **D.** Bilaterally Symmetrical Spores *(Calostoma cinnabaria)*; **E.** Asymmetrical Spores *(Coprinus silvatious)*.

does not correspond to the longitudinal axis of the spore. In all basidiocarps in which the spores are not forcibly ejected and from which spore prints can not be obtained (notably the Gasteromycetes), the spore attachment is called **Orthotropic** (Fig. 28B). In orthotropic spore attachment, the longitudinal axis of the sterigma corresponds to that of the spore. In many secotiaceous relatives of the agarics although the spores are not forcibly discharged, they are nevertheless heterotropic.

3. Spore Symmetry

If a spore when viewed in face, side or end views can be divided into mirror images along an imaginary line, the spore is considered **Symmetrical**. If the spore can not be divided into mirror images, the spore is considered **Asymmetrical** (Fig. 28E). Two types of symmetrical spores are recognized: 1) the spore can be divided into equal halves along only one line; this type of spore is considered **Bilaterally Symmetrical** (Fig. 28D). 2) the spore can be divided into mirror images along several lines; this type of spore is considered **Radially Symmetrical** (Fig. 28C). When determining the symmetry of a spore, it is particularly important to identify the view of the spore which is being observed since different views can present different types of symmetry. For example, the spores in Figure 000 are bilaterally symmetrical in face view, asymmetrical in side view and radially symmetrical in end view.

Spore symmetry can be determined from the measurements of a spore as seen in side or face view. For example, **Radially Symmetrical** spores usually have a length minus width (L − W) measurement of from $0.0 − 1.5 (−1.9)\mu m$ or a length divided by width (L/W) from $1.0 − 1.24\mu m$ (the quotient is often expressed as Q). These spores are often called **Isodiametric** spores. Spores which have a L − W measurement of more than $2.0\mu m$ or a Q greater than 1.25 are often called **Heterodiametric** spores. Heterodiametric spores can be further subdivided into categories based on the shape of the spore. For example, if the length of a spore is just barely longer than the width so that the spore is almost ovate, the spores are called **Heterodiametric-Ovate** (the Q of these spores ranges from $1.25 − 1.5$). Or if the spores are elliptical to cylindrical in shape; such spores are called **Heterodiametric-Elliptical** (or **Cylindrical**) and have a Q of 1.6 or more.

Angular spores can likewise be isodiametric or heterodiametric. The general outline of the spore (not including every angle or nodule) can be used to describe shape. Thus an isodiametric (and angular) spore is more or less round in outline. The longest measurement is the length and the width is a corresponding measurement perpendicular to the length. Types of angular spores are beyond the scope of this book. Pegler and Young (1977) describe morphology of angular spores admirably.

Recent studies using the electron microscope have revealed the complexities of basidiospore walls (see Singer, 1975). These discoveries are extremely important in determining evolutionary relationships among agarics and boletes. A new terminology is evolving which corresponds to older terms applied to the wall and internal structures. For most routine work in agaricology the more precise terminology is impractical. The difficulty arises from the fact that details of the spore wall are at the limits of the resolving power of the light microscope. The spore wall of the most complex basidiospore is composed of five parts. These are as follows: 1) an outer layer, called the **Perisporium** (Fig. 29A), which is non-pigmented and usually envelops the spore like a bag which may disappear (see *Coprinus narcoticus* and its allies); 2) the **Exosporium** (Fig. 29B), which usually is not pigmented and can often be distinguished chemically from the surrounding layers; 3) the **Episporium** (Fig. 29C) which is a continuation of the outer wall layer of the sterigma and basidium. It is usually the thickest layer thereby providing structural support; 4) the **Mesosporium** (Fig. 29D), a barely distinguishable and delicate structure; 5) the **Endosporium** (Fig. 29E) which can vary from very thick (in which case it can then be divided into an inner and outer portion) *to* seemingly or truly absent (e.g. so called thin-walled or **Monostratous** spore walls of *Tubaria* (Pl. XXXII A) have no endosporium; the spores frequently collapse when placed in liquid). The presence or absence of any of these layers varies from taxa to taxa. Since the origin of the spore ornamentation also varies, the layers can not be presumed homologous. Singer (1975) summarizes the observations made in Clemençon (1970) and in Pegler and Young (1971) and should be referred to for more detailed study.

At the apical end of some spores, there appears to be a pore or hole in the spore wall; this area is called an **Apical (Germ) Pore** or more commonly simply the **Germ-pore** (Pl. XXIV A,D). Actually the germ-pore is a thin spot in the wall through which the spore may germinate; furthermore, the pore may be oblique or centered with respect to the spore axis. If the wall thinning forms a convex protrusion, it is termed a **Callus** as in *Psathyrella (Lacrymaria) rigidipes*.

Sometimes the oily or refractive contents of a spore will give the false impression that a spore is punctate or otherwise ornamented. Spores with obvious oil globules are said to be **Guttulate** (Pl. XXIV B).

4. Spore Size

Two measurements are usually taken when determining spore size, the length of the spore and the width of the spore; if possible, these measurements should be taken from a spore deposit to insure measuring mature spores. Spores are usually measured in face and/or side views since differences in measurements of spores seen in end view usually are not noticeable. It is particularly important to indicate the view of the spore from which the measurements have been taken; for example the length of an asymmetrical spore will be the same in both side and face views but the width is likely to be different in those views.

The range of spore size as well as the average spore size should be determined. Find the range of spore size based on the majority of spores observed but do not include the smallest or largest spores seen in the field of view. Measurements are taken and indicated in an arithmetical manner; for example, if the smallest spore in a field was 7.5μm long and the largest was 14μm but most spores were between 9 and 12μm the spore range would be indicated as (7.5-) 9-12 (-14)μm. The average spore size is particularly important in many genera of agarics, eg. *Cortinarius* and *Leptonia*. If working with spores from a freshly made spore print, 10-15 spores need to be measured in a thick fleshed agaric but preferably up to 25 for a thin-fleshed agaric (eg. *Conocybe*). If working with spores from herbarium material measure at least 20-25 spores, and in cases where a wide variation is apparent use up to 50.

Once the range of spore size has been determined, it is useful to determine the spore **Quotient** (Q). The average spore quotient from any sample is called E. Furthermore some agaricologists determine the range and average **Difference** of the spore (length minus width or diameter) (L-W or L-D). These arithmetical values can sometimes provide an indication of the shape. For example, in Bas' work on *Amanita* (1969), shapes are defined as follows:

globose	Q = 1.01-1.05	ellipsoid	Q = 1.30-1.60
subglobose	Q = 1.05-1.15	elongate(=oblong)	Q = 1.60-2.0
broadly ellipsoid	Q = 1.15-1.30	cylindric	Q = 2.0-3.0
		bacciliform	Q > 3.0

Spore measurements usually include the ornamentation but not the apiculus except for those spores which have extremely large ornamented surfaces as in the Russulaceae and in some species of *Gomphus* or *Ramaria*. In these latter examples, the ornamentation itself is measured and the spore size is usually indicated exclusive of ornamentation.

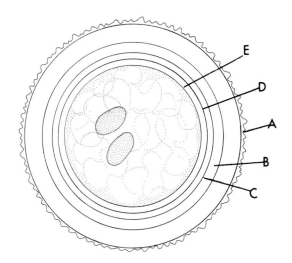

FIG. 29. **Spore Wall. A.** Perisporium; **B.** Exosporium; **C.** Episporium; **D.** Mesosporium; **E.** Endosporium.

5. Spore Ornamentation

An ornamented spore is characterized by an outgrowth of some part of the spore wall which results in the ornamentation. The electron microscope has shown that the ornamentation of a spore can originate from any layer of the spore wall. Ornamentations which appear similar under the light microscope can originate from different layers of the spore wall. However, at present these differences do not hinder describing spores when studying the microscopic features of agarics or boletes.

As can be expected from any man-made attempt to categorize biological organisms, more than one term has evolved to describe a similar type of ornamentation. Furthermore, since organisms mature at different rates, the spore ornamentation can vary with the age and the maturity of the basidiocarp; consequently more than one term will be used to describe spore ornamentation within a species. Terms used to describe spore ornamentation are usually different from those used to describe shape. But if ornamentation ceases to be superficial it begins to change the outline of a spore. For example, as ridges give way to angles, a single term applies to both shape and ornamentation.

In most instances, spores are ornamented over their entire surface; exceptions occur, as in the majority of species of *Galerina* for example, in which the suprahilar plage or disc is not ornamented. It appears as a smooth area on the dorsal side of the spore.

Some spores appear ornamented in optical section but the outline of the spore is perfectly smooth; such spores are called **Falsely Echinulate** or **Ganodermoid** (after the genus *Ganoderma*) (Fig. 31G; Pl. XXII D). In these spores, the ornamentations originate from the endosporium or the episporium but do not penetrate through the exosporium.

In the simplest kind of ornamentation, the outgrowths are so minute as to appear almost non-existent. If such ornamentations are more or less equidistant, the spore is called **Punctate** (Fig. 30A; Pl. XXIV A) or **Punctate-roughened** (as in *Cortinarius punctatus*). Three different sets of terminology have evolved describing elaborations on the shape of those individual ornamentations: ornamentations that are round in outline; ornamentations that are pointed in outline; and ornamentations that follow lines or ridges.

Rounded Ornamentations:
Abundant and close together:
Wrinkled: The ornamentations are so abundant
and so close together that each outgrowth appears confluent with the next. When the wrinkles appear fine, the spore is called **Rugulose** whereas if the wrinkles are coarse, the spore is called **Rugose.**
More or Less Equidistant From Each Other:
Verruculose: The outgrowths are moderate in size.
Verrucose (Fig. 30B): The outgrowths are a bit more prominent (as in *Horakia verrucospora*).
Warty: The outgrowths are still larger.

104

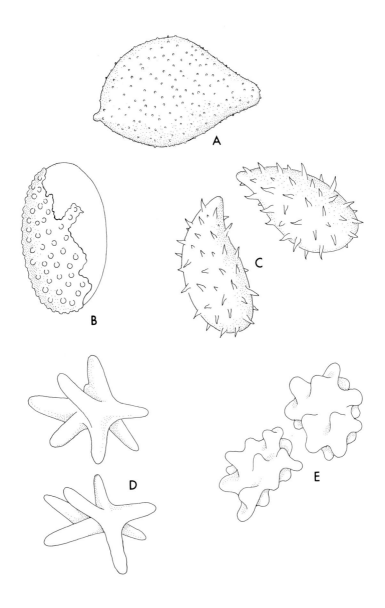

FIG. 30. **Spore Ornamentation I. A.** Punctate (*Descolea flavo-annulata*); **B.** Verrucose; **C.** Spinose (*Ramaria* sp.); **D.** Stellate (*Inocybe insignis*); **E.** Nodulose (*Inocybe* sp.).

Tuberculate (Pl. XXII A): The outgrowths are so prominent as to be extremely obvious; frequently the outgrowths will measure more than 1.0μm.
Nodulose (Fig. 30E, 36G; Pl. XXV B): The outgrowths are very large and make the spore appear as if decorated by knobs (as in *Conocybe nodulosospora*).
Stellate (Fig. 30D, 36F): The outgrowths are very prominent so that the spore appears star-shaped. Sometimes the word **Asteriform** (as in *Clitocybe asterospora*) is used for spores that are star-shaped but the projections are not as elongate as in stellate spores.

Ridged Ornamentations:
Striate (Fig. 31D): The ridges are rather small.
Ribbed (subalate) (Fig. 31E): The ridges are moderate in size.
Costate (Fig. 31F): The ridges are quite large, usually 1μm or more (as in *Strobilomyces costatisporus*).
Pterate (or **Alate**): The ridges are so large so that they make the spore wing-like in appearance (as in *Lactarius pterosporus*).

Pointed Ornamentations:
Asperulate (Fig. 31A): The spore appears roughened with tiny, small points (as in *Lepiota asperula*). Be careful, however, since this same term can be applied to spores that are roughened with small warts, eg. *Melanoleuca* where the warts are amyloid.
Echinulate (or **Spinulose**): The points are moderate in size (as in *Gymnopilus echinulisporus*).
Echinate (or **Spinose**) (Fig. 30C; 31B): The points are quite large (as in *Crepidotus echinosporus*).
Aculeate (Fig. 31C): The spines are very sharp pointed.

Striate Ornamentations:
The ornamentation may be randomly distributed or show some organization into lines called **Striae** which may be formed by the joining of several distinct outgrowths. If these striate-spores also have tubercles or large warts visible as ornamentations, they are called **Tuberculate-striate**. Often the striae are inter-connected and therefore form a net; such ornamented spores are called **Reticulate** (Fig. 32A; Pl. XXII C). Finally if the striae are enlarged into ridges as well as connected into a net, the spores are called **Lacunose** (Fig. 32B).
Until this point, spore ornamentation has been described regardless of the layer of the spore wall from which it originated. Two terms describe ornamentations originating from the outermost layer of the spore wall, the perisporium. If the perisporium forms a partial envelope or bag around the spore, the spore is called **Calyptrate** (Fig. 32C; Pl. XXIII D) (as in *Galerina calyptrospora*). If the perisporium completely surrounds the spore, the spores are called **Utriculate** (Fig. 32D).
In some agarics, the spore appears ornamented in one view and either unornamented or differently ornamented in the other view. For example, in the genus *Clitopilus* ((Fig. 32E; Pl. XXII B), the spore is longitudinally striate in side and face view but in end views the striae appear as angles. The striae are in fact pronounced furrows, so in end-view the spore appears angular. In *Rhodocybe* (Fig. 32F), spores are angular in end view but rugose in side or face views .

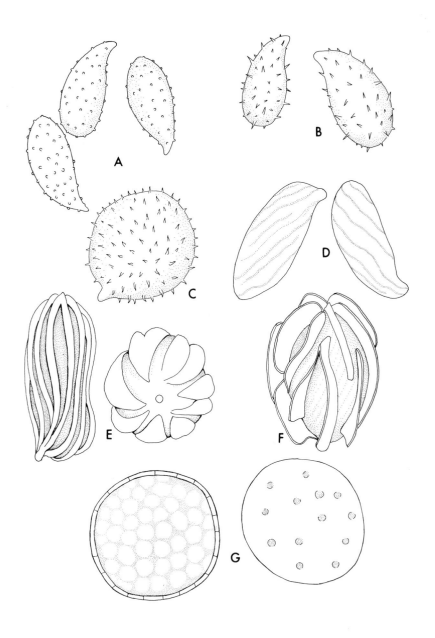

FIG. 31. **Spore Ornamentation II. A.** Asperulate (*Clavaria* sp.); **B.** Echinate (*Ramaria* sp.); **C.** Aculeate (*Laccaria laccata*); **D.** Striate (*Ramaria* sp.); **E.** Ribbed (*Boletellus* sp.); **F.** Costate (*Strobilomyces costatispora*); **G.** Falsely Echinulate (*Fayodia bisphaerigera*).

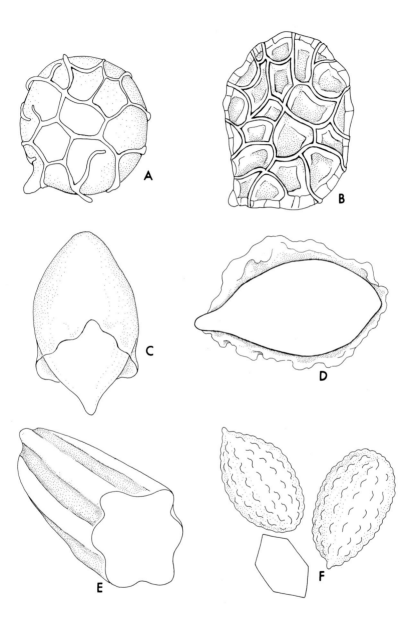

FIG. 32. **Spore Ornamentation III. A.** Reticulate (*Lactarius fuliginosus*); **B.** Lacunose (*Strobilomyces floccopus*), **C.** Calyptrate (*Galerina turfosa*), **D.** Utriculate (*Hymenogaster thwaitesii*); **E.** *Clitopilus* Spore (*Clitopilus prunulus*); **F.** *Rhodocybe* Spore (*Rohdocybe caelata*).

6. Spore Shape

A. INTRODUCTORY REMARKS

Terminology describing spore shape is confusing partly because of imprecise application in the literature and partly because we are studying biological entities only a few microns in length. We suggest using a bit of modeling clay to help imagine the shapes in three dimensions.

Practically speaking, we measure length and width of a spore regularly and the breadth only infrequently. Imagine a spore shaped like an ordinary almond. You could measure its length, width and breadth with the breadth being its thickness. Only a few basidiospores are obviously compressed like an almond but many assume the almond shape in some view (as in *Crepidotus amygdalosporus*).

Three terms, ovoid, elliptic and round are frequently misused. The term ovoid means shaped like an egg, with the distal end (away from point of attachment to the basidium) being wider and broader than the proximal end (at the point of attachment to the basidium). No matter how you roll the spore under the microscope it is egg-shaped (except in end view). The word ovoid describes a 3 dimensional figure, while ovate refers to a shape in two dimensions (i.e. an optical section). Likewise elliptic refers to a shape in optical section and ellipsoid refers to 3 dimensional objects. Ovate and ovoid are frequently used synonomously or ovoid is used to denote a spore not quite egg-shaped but close to it. Although we make these distinctions here, the terms are not rigorously applied in the literature.

Also, the widely used term elliptic, is not technically precise. In geometry any oblique plane passed through a cone forms an ellipse. The shape can be long and cucumber-like to one falling just short of a perfect circle. In practice, elliptic refers to a shape with roughly the same length/width proportions of an egg, but both ends are of equal size and taper.

Round is an ideal shape which heterotropic spores (see above under *spore attachment*) rarely attain by virtue of their mode of liberation. Globose is not identical to round because it refers to the shape of a sphere, hence not quite but almost round. Since we are talking of almost imperceptible differences, the terms are applied synonomously by most authors. The widely accepted term is subglobose, intended to convey the idea that a majority of the spores are slightly longer than broad.

To describe intermediate shapes use compound forms, such as elliptic-oblong. This term indicates the spore is more or less oblong but tends to be somewhat elliptic (the ends are not as blunt as in a truly oblong spore). The modifier sub- can be used to indicate shapes which almost fit the term (i.e. sub-cylindric = almost cylindric).

The shape of a spore is its outline as seen in one view, usually the face or the side view. Consequently a spore can assume different shapes when seen in different views; eg. the spores of *Coprinus cordisporus* are elliptical in side view, cordate in face view and oblong in end view, whereas the spores of *Cystoagaricus* are cordate in face view and elliptical in side and end views.

B. TERMINOLOGY

It is quite important when distinguishing the shape of a spore to determine the apical end from the basal end of the spore. The apical end may be shaped differently from the base. Moreover, it may be rounded, flattened or truly squared off; in the latter case spores are called **Truncate** (Pl. XXXIII C, XXIV D). Numerous terms apply to spore shape; these can best be distinguished from each other when placed on a continuum. The starting point for such a continuum is the perfectly round spore which is called **Spherical** or **Globose** (Fig. 33A). A spore that is nearly round is called **Subspherical** or **Subglobose** (Fig. 33B)(as in *Cyphelliopsis subglobispora* or in *Mniopetalum globisporum* or *Mycena globispora*).

The subglobose spore can either be altered in the middle, in which case the ends of the spore are similar, or it can be altered more towards one end than the other in which case the apical and basal views are different. Globose and subglobose spores are for all practical purposes radially symmetrical from all views. Furthermore they are also equilateral from all views which means that the sides are identical in appearance.

All spores can be derived from subglobose spores by altering the symmetry of the spore. If the spore is bilaterally symmetrical, the sides of the spore will be identical; such spores can be considered **Equilateral**. If the spore is asymmetrical, the spore will appear lopsided since the sides are dissimilar; such spores are considered **Inequilateral**.

C. EQUILATERAL SPORES

Equilateral spores can vary in the following manner: the spore can not be tapered at all, or both ends can be tapered, or one end can be tapered and the other can not.

Non-Tapered Equilateral Spores:

Elliptic (Ellipsoid) (Fig. 33C; Pl. XXIII A,B,C, XXIV A,B,D): The simplest equilateral spore in which the ends are rounded and the sides are curved (as in *Pleuromycenula ellipsoidea*).

Lentiform (Lenticular): A spore which is broader than and not as long as an ellipsoid spore; lens-shaped.

Oblong (Fig. 33D): The sides are almost parallel, the ends squarish and the length/width ratio is about 2-3 (as in *Marasmiellus oblongispora*).

Cylindric (Fig. 33E): The sides are more or less parallel and the length/width ratio is 4-6 (as in *Calyptella cylindrospora*).

Bacciliform (Fig. 33F): The sides are parallel, the ends more or less roundish and the length/width ratio is 7-8; uncommon in North American agarics.

Equilateral Spores with Both Ends Tapered:

Fusiform (Fig. 33G): The spore is fairly broad in the middle and tapered to both ends, like a spindle (as in *Cortinarius fusiformis*).

110

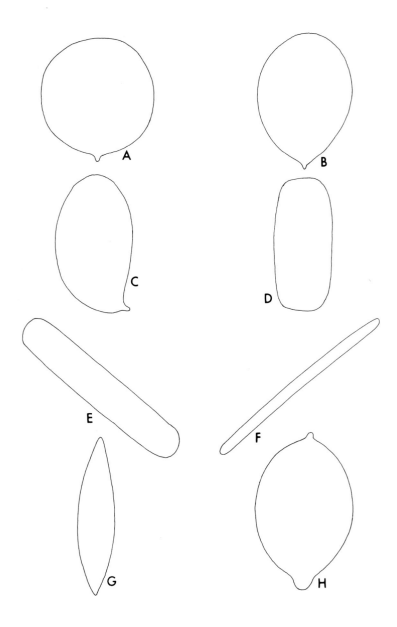

FIG. 33. **Spore Shape I. A.** Globose; **B.** Sublobose; **C.** Elliptical (*Clitocybe* sp.); **D.** Oblong; **E.** Cylindrical; **F.** Bacilliform; **G.** Fusiform; Citriniform (*Phaeocollybia* sp.).

Aciculiform: The spore is fairly narrow in the middle and sharply pointed at both ends, like a needle.

Naviculate (Fig. 34E): The spore is broader at one end, but both ends are essentially tapered.

Citriniform (Limoniform) (Fig. 33H): The very ends of the spore are tapered so that they appear beak-like, lemon-shaped.

Equilateral Spores with One End Tapered:

In most spores, the apical or distal end of the spore is broader and the spore narrows toward the basal end where the hilar appendage is located. When a spore is broader at the basal end and narrows towards the apical end, the prefix **Ob-** is used before any of the following terms.

Dacryoid (Lachryform or **Lacrymoid)** (Fig. 34C): The spore is almost globose except for tapering just at one end, like a tear (tear-shaped).

Ovate (Oval) (Fig. 34A; Pl. XXII A,C,D, XXIII A): The spore is rounded on both ends but the ends are unequal in width, therefore the taper is quite gradual, like an egg (=ovum) (egg-shaped).

Pyriform (Fig. 34B): The spore is more elongate as well as more tapered at the apiculate end than an oval spore, like a pear (pear-shaped).

Amygdaliform (Fig. 34D; Pl. XXIV A): Not as tapered as a pyriform spore, like an almond (almond-shaped) (as in *Crepidotus amygdalosporus*).

Pruniform: Broader than an amygdaliform spore but tapered in a similar fashion, like a prune (prune-shaped).

Naviculate (Fig. 34E): Bullet shaped or projectile – shaped.

Unusual Equilateral Spores:

Two unusual spore shapes are heart-shaped or **Cordate** (Fig.34F) (as in *Psilocybe cordisporus*) and **Cuneate** or wedge-shaped. These spores are flattened in end as well as profile view.

D. INEQUILATERAL SPORES

Allantoid (Fig. 35A): A cylindric spore with one bend, like a sausage (sausage-shaped).

Phaseoliform (Fig. 35C): A curved spore in the shape of a french or scarlet runner bean.

Reniform: A curved spore, in the shape of a kidney bean.

Sigmoid (Fig. 35B): A bacciliform spore with two bends.

Amphicoeious (Fig. 35D): A more or less phaseoliform spore in which the ventral (swollen) side becomes depressed to concave.

Subfusiform (Fig. 35E; Pl. XXIV C): A spore which is elongate and unequally tapered at one end and rounded at the other.

Pip-shaped (Fig. 35F): Essentially dacryoid but the tapered end is bent.

Rostrate (Fig. 35G): Distinctly beaked, particularly at the distal end; the taper is pronounced and protrudes like a beak. If the beak is big, the spore is called **Rostrate** and **Rostrulate** if it is small.

112

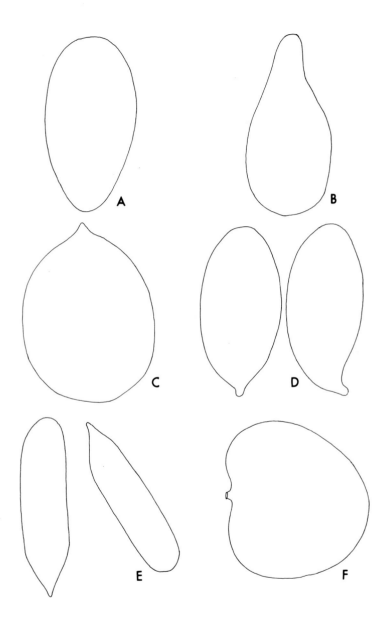

FIG. 34. **Spore Shape II. A.** Ovate; **B.** Pyriform; **C.** Dacryoid (*Hydnum* Sp.); **D.** Amygdaliform (*Cortinarius* sp.); **E.** Naviculate (*Mycena paucilamellata*); **F.** Cordate (*Psathyrella hirsutosquamulosa*).

113

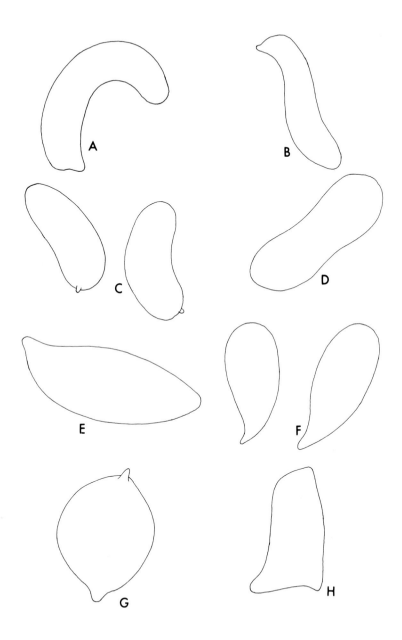

FIG. 35. **Spore Shape III. A.** Allantoid (*Pleurotus* sp.); **B.** Sigmoid, (*Clavaria* sp.); **C.** Phaseoliform (*Inocybe* sp.); **D.** Amphicoelous (*Inocybe* sp.); **E.** Subfusiform (*Clavaria* sp.), **F.** Pip-shaped (*Collybia* sp.); **G.** Rostrate (*Phaeocollybia* sp.); **H.** Projectile-shaped (*Lepiota* sp.).

Many agarics possess spores in which the outline of the spore is not rounded but in the form of angles (as in *Crepidotus angulosus*). If the outline of one face or side of an angular spore has 4 angles, it is called **Quadrate** (Fig. 36A; Pl. XXV D) or square-shaped. A cube-shaped spore with six equal faces is termed **Rhomboid** (Fig. 36B; Pl. XXV D) (as in *Leptonia rhombispora*). Some faces of an angular spore are very slightly six-angled and this shape is termed simply **Hexagonal** (Fig. 36C). When there are more than 6 sides and angles and the spore is irregular in shape, it is usually called **Polygonal** (Fig. 36D; Pl. XXV C). In these more complicated shapes the base of the spore must be carefully observed to determine how the apiculus is attached.

In some agarics the angles are enlarged into more or less outgrowths at which time the spore is called **Nodulose** (Fig. 36G, 30E; Pl. XXV B) or wavy nodulose as in *Pouzarella*. When the outgrowths are more elongated, either the spore is called **Prismatic** (Fig. 36E; Pl. XXV A) if it is shaped like a prism or it is called **Stellate** (Fig. 30D, 36F) if it is shaped like a star. Many of these angular shapes can be found in the Rhodophyllaceae. See Pegler and Young (1971, 1977).

C. CHEMICAL REACTIONS OF SPORES

The most common chemicals used when studying spores are Melzer's reagent, cresyl blue and cotton blue. The names for spores which react with these reagents are as follows:

Amyloid (Pl. XXII A,C): Spores (as in *Lentinellus*) or spore ornamentations (as in *Russula, Lactarius* and *Melanoleuca*) which turn blue or black in Melzer's.

Dextrinoid (Pseudoamyloid): Spores which turn reddish- or purplish brown in Melzer's.

Inamyloid: Spores which do not react with Melzer's reagent and therefore appear yellow (the natural color of the reagent) or hyaline.

Metachromatic: The term applied to spores in which one or more parts of the wall turn red when placed in cresyl blue.

Cyanophilous or **Cyanophilic**: Spores in which the wall of the spores turns a more dark color of blue than the interior. When such a reaction *does not* occur, the spore is called **Acyanophilous** or **Acyanophilic**.

Some features of spores can be seen better when mounted in a particular chemical. These are:

1. The **Suprahilar Plage** can best be seen by washing the spores in a 50% aqueous solution of chloralhydrate and then mounting the spore in 10% ammonium hydroxide.

2. The **Apical Germ Pore** can best be seen using 1% cresyl blue.

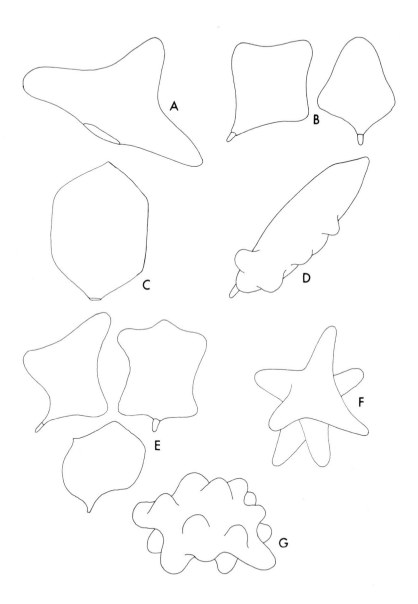

FIG. 36. **Spore Shape IV. A.** Quadrate; **B.** Rhomboid; **C.** Hexagonal (*Psilocybe aerugineo-maculans*); **D,** Polygonal (*Inocybe* sp.); **E.** Prismatic; **F.** Stellate (*Inocybe insignis*); **G.** Nodulose (*Inocybe* sp.).

116

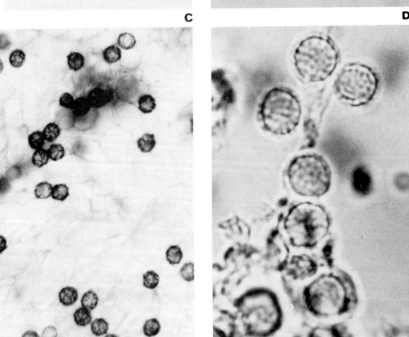

PL. XXII. **Basidiospores 1. A.** Tuberculate, Amyloid, Ovate (*Macowanites americanum*); **B.** *Clitopilus prunulus*; angular in end view, longitudinally striate in side view. **C.** Tuberculate-Reticulate, Amyloid, Ovate (*Lactaruis fuliginosus*); **D.** Falsely Echinulate, Ovate (*Fayodia bisphaerigera*).

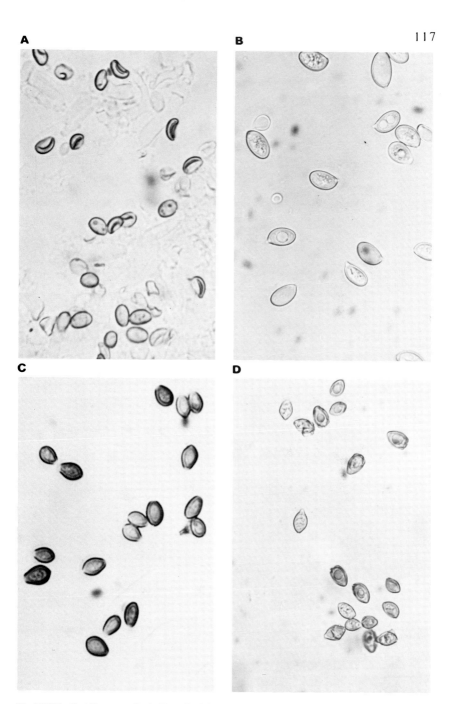

PL. XXIII. **Basidiospores 2. A.** Broadly Elliptic to Ovate, Smooth; Collapsed due to Monostratous Wall (*Tubaria pellucida*); **B.** Elliptic with distinct hilar appendage, Smooth (*Volvariella speciosa*); **C.** Subovate to Elliptic, broadly truncate, Smooth (*Coprinus micaceus*); **D.** Slightly inequilateral in profile view, narrowly ovate in face view, calyptrate (*Galerina allospora*).

118

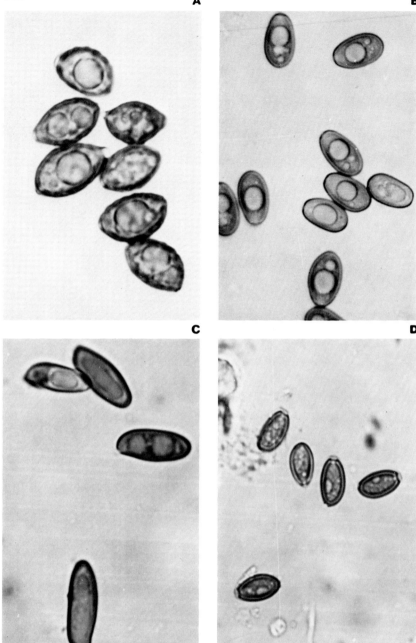

PL. XXIV. **Basidiospores 3. A.** Broadly Elliptical to Slightly Amygdaliform, Punctate and with an Apical Pore (*Panaeolina foenescii*). **B.** Elliptical, Smooth (note oil droplets within spores) (*Bolbitius vitellinus*); **C.** Subfusiform, Smooth, (note hilar appendage in spore nearest bottom) (*Gomphidius subroseus*); **D.** Elliptical, Smooth, Truncate due to Apical Pore (*Stropharia ambigua*).

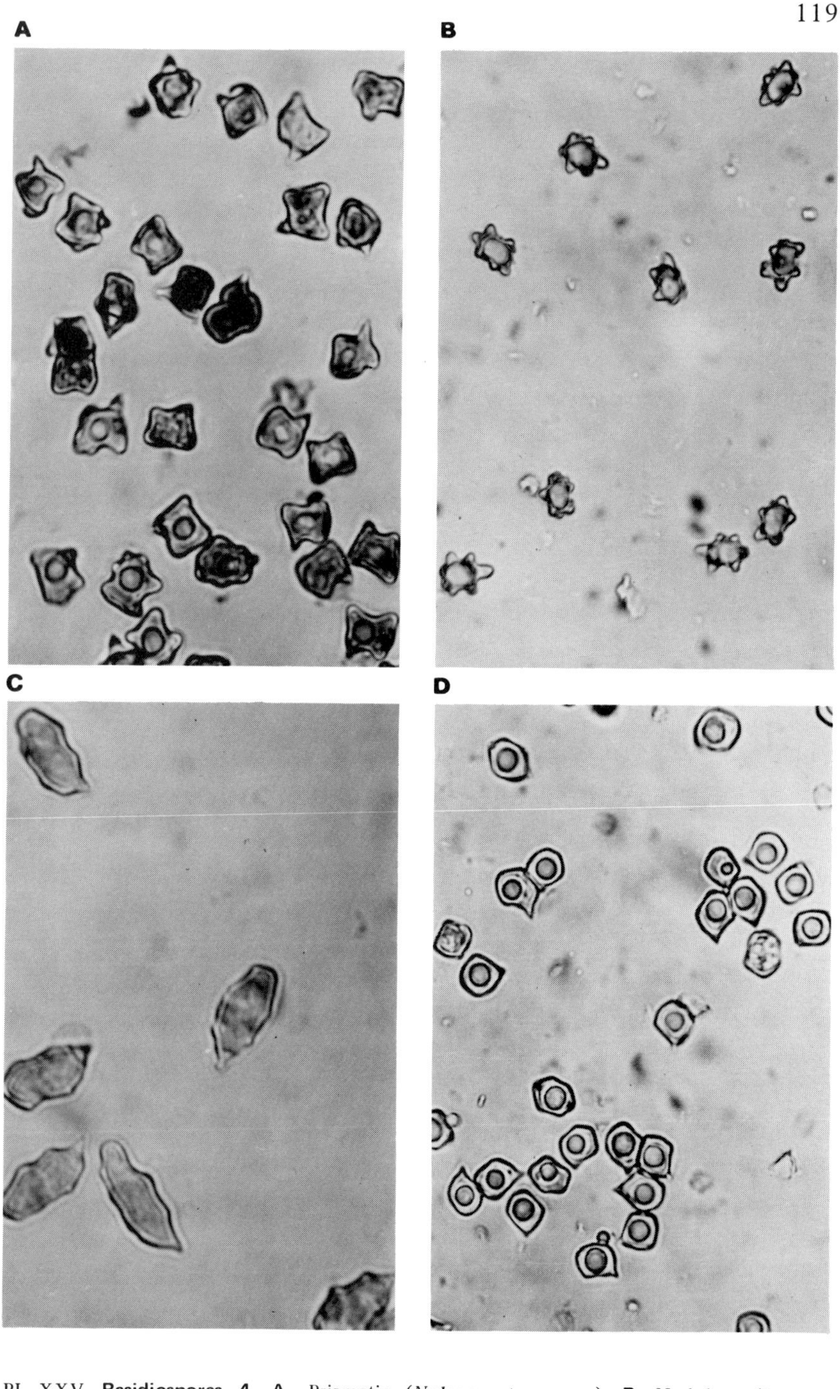

PL. XXV. **Basidiospores 4. A.** Prismatic (*Nolanea staurospoa*); **B.** Nodulose (*Inocybe praetervisa*); **C.** Polygonal (*Pouzarurella dysthales*); **D.** Rhomboid (Quadrate in any view) (*Leptonia watsoni*).

120

LITERATURE CITED

Bas, C. 1969. Morphology and subdivision of Amanita and a monograph of its section Lepidella. *Persoonia* 5:285-579.

Buller, A. H. R. 1924. *Researches On Fungi*. Vol. 3, 611pp.

Clemençon, H. 1970. Bau der Wände der Basidiosporen und ein Vorschlag zur Bennenung ihrer Schichten. *Zeitschr Pilzk*. 36: 113-133.

Corner, E. J. H. 1932. The fruitbody of *Polystictus xanthopus* Fr. *Ann. Botany (London)* 46: 71-111.

—————. 1966. A monograph of Cantharelloid fungi. *Annls. Bot. Mem. 2*.

Fayod, V. 1889. Prodrome d'une histoire naturelle des Agaricinés. *Annls. Sci. Nat., Bot. Sér*. 7,9: 181-411.

Gäumann, E. A. and F. L. Wynd. 1952. *The Fungi. A Description of Their Morphological Features and Evolutionary Development*. Hafner, New York. 420pp.

Grund, D. W. and C. D. Marr. 1965. New methods for demonstrating carminophilous granulation. *Mycologia*. 57: 583-587.

Henderson, D. M., P. D. Orton and R. Watling. 1969. *British Fungus Flora. Agarics and Boleti. Introduction*. Edinburgh.

Kühner, R. and H. Romagnesi. 1953. *Flore Analytique des Champignons Supérieurs (Agarics, Bolets, Chanterelles)*. Paris: Masson. 556pp.

Lentz, P. A. 1954. Modified hyphae of Hymenomycetes. *Bot. Rev.* 20: 135-199.

Locquin, M. 1953. Reserches sur l'organisation et le développement des Agarics, des Bolets et des Clavaires. *Bull. Soc. Mycol. Fr.* 69:389-402.

Lohwag, H. 1941. *Anatomie der Asco- und Basidiomyceten*. Berlin. (Nachdruck, 1965, Berlin).

Palmer, J. T. 1955. Observations on Gasteromycetes. 1-3. *Trans. Brit. Mycol. Soc.* 38:317-334.

Pegler, D. N. and T. W. K. Young. 1971. Basidiospore Morphology in the Agaricales. *Beih. Nova Hedwigia*. 35.

_____. 1977. Spore Form and Phylogeny of Entolomataceae. (Agaricales). *Sydowia*. (In Press)

Romagnesi, H. 1944. La Cystide chez les Agaricacées. *Rev. Mycol.* (N. S.) 9: Suppl. 4-21.

Singer, R. 1975. *Agaricales in Modern Taxonomy*. Ed. 3. A. R. Gantner Verlag, Germany.

Smith, A. H. 1949. *Mushrooms in Their Natural Habitats*. Sawyers, Inc. 626pp.

_____. 1966. The Hyphal structure of the Basidiocarp. in *Fungi. An Advance Treatise. II. The Fungal Organism.* C. W. Ainsworth and A. S. Sussman, Eds. Academic Press, N. Y. 805pp.

Snell, W. H. and E. A. Dick. 1957. *A Glossary of Mycology*. Harvard Univ. Press, Cambridge. 169pp.

Talbot, P. H. B. 1954. Micromorphology of the lower Hymenomycetes. *Bothalia* 6: 249-299.

Webster, J. 1970. *Introduction to Fungi*. Univ. Press, Cambridge. 424pp.

122

GLOSSARY, INDEX AND EXAMPLES OF FEATURES

The following is an alphabetized list of terms used in this book and includes some words that may be encountered in agaricological works but not in this work. After each word may be found some comments, a list of commonly encountered mushrooms (or other fungi) that can be used to demonstrate the feature listed, or a page reference (* equals illustration page). If no page reference follows the word, or the comments, the term will not be found elsewhere in this book. To find the chapter and subchapter headings check the table of contents.

ABAXIAL (Dorsal) 96.

ACANTHOPHYSIS. Not found in the Agaricales but closely approached in the cheilo- and pileocystidia of *Mycena brownii* and *M. corticola.* Also found in the acanthophysoid cystidia of *Mycena citrinomarginata, M. galericulata, M. fumosiavellanea* and *M. epipterygia.* 74, 75*.

ACICULATE. (=Acicular) 78, 79*.

ACICULIFORM. 111.

ACICULAR. *Mycena griseovirdis, M. longiseta* (Tops of appendages of cheilocystidia), *M. tenerrima* (Tops of appendages of cheilocystidia); *Pluteus thomsonii* (Tip of cystidia); *Russula herterophylla* (Pileipellis units); *Coprinus auricomus* and *Psathyrella conopilea* (Setoid cells in pileipellis). 78.

ACULEATE. *Laccaria laccata, L. tortilis* (Basidiospores); *Pouzarella nodospora* (Caulocystidia), *Naucoria escharoides* (Apex of pileocystidia). 75*, 78, 79*, 105, 106*.

ACUMINATE. *Macrocystidia cucumis, Melanoleuca* sp., *Psathyrella squamosa, Mycena alcalina, M. abramsii, M. sanguinolenta* (Cheilo- pleuro- and caulocystidia). 77*, 78.

ACUTE. Pointed; see acicular, aculeate, and acuminate. 76, 88*.

ACYANOPHILIC. 114.

ACYANOPHILOUS. 114.

ADAXIAL (=Ventral). 96.

AEQUIHYMENIIFEROUS. Developing equally all over the surface. Characteristic of all agaric genera except *Coprinus*. 90.

ALATE (=Pterate). *Lactarius pterosporus, L. ruginosus; Russula laurocerasi* (Basidiospores). 105.

ALLANTOID. *Panellus stypticus, P. serotinus, Phyllotopsis nidulans* (long phaseoliform) (Basidiospores). 111, 113*.

AMPHICOELOUS. *Inocybe fastigiata, Ramaria longispora, Conocybe brunnea* (Basidiospores). 111, 113*.

AMPHIMITIC. Composed of generative and binding hyphae. *Laetiporus sulphureus, Polyporus squamosus,* some tropical Pleurotaceae. 30.

AMPULLATE (=Ampulliform). 76.

AMPULLIFORM. *Galerina ampullaecystis, G. sideroides, G. pseudocamerina, Agrocybe pediades* (Cheilocystidia). 76, 78.

AMYGDALIFORM. *Naucoria celluloderma, N. escharioides, Hebeloma crustuliniforme, Agrocybe praecox* (Basidiospores). 111, 112*, 118*.

AMYLOID. *Leucopaxillus* (smooth Basidiospores), *Leucopaxillus and Melanoleuca* (Ornamentation of the spores), *Lactarius, Russula, Melanoleuca melaleuca, Mycena galericulata* (Basidiospores); *Chroogomphus rutilis* (Hyphae); *Boletus calopus* (Septa); *Psathyrella cotonea* (Cystidia). 25, 114, 116*.

ANGULAR. *Inocybe clypeus* group, *Sarcodon, Hydnellum,* many Rhodophylloid agarics (Basidiospores). 114, 116*.

APEX. 96, 98*.

APICAL GERM PORE. *Stropharia ambigua, S. semiglobata, Psilocybe semilanceata, Kuhneromyces mutabilis, Conocybe tenera, Bolbitius vitellinus, Coprinus sassii, C. ephemerus, C. flocculosus, C. hexagonosporus, C. bisporus, C. congreatus, C. plicatilis, C. comatus, C. micaceus, Psathyrella coprophila* (oblique); *Panaeolina foenisecii* (central). 96, 98*, 101, 114, 118*.

APICULUS. Characteristic of all agarics. 97, 98*.

APPENDAGES. *Agrocybe arvalis (Pleurocystidia); Mycena galericulata, M. lineata, M. subincarnata (Cystidia); Flammulina velutipes* (elements of the pileipellis); *Pleurotellus patelloides* (Cystidia). (See Diverticulate or rod-like outgrowths).

APPLANATION. Suprahilar disc or plage; see species of *Galerina*.

ASEPTATE. Without septa. Hyphae of the common bread mold. Vascular hyphae in *Boletus edulis*. Gloeocystidial elements in *Lentinellus*. Excretory hyphae in *Pholiota* and *Stropharia*. 32.

ASPERULATE. *Crepidotus variabilis*, *C. luteolus*, *Myxomphalia maura*, *Melanoleuca* (with Melzer's), *Lepiota asperula*, *Tylopilus gracilis*, (Basidiospores). 105, 106*

ASSYMMETRICAL SPORES. 99*, 100.

ASTERIFORM. *Inocybe asterospora*, *Clitocybe asterospora*. (Basidiospores). 105.

ASTEROID. *Tricholoma goniospermum*, *Nolanea staurospora* (Basidiospores). 105.

ASTEROPHYSIS. Stellate hyphal end characteristic of tramal and hymenium cells in *Asterostroma*. 74, 75*.

ASTEROSTROMELLOID. (c.f. dichophysoid).

ASTROSETAE. (see Asterophysis).

BACCIFORM. Shaped like a berry.

BACCILIFORM. Amanita cylindrospora. 109, 110*.

BARBELLATE (= Cornuate).

BASE OF SPORE. 96, 98*.

BASIDIUM. 89-93 (84*, 92-93*, 98*)

BASIDIOSPORES. 94-114 (97-99*, 102*, 104*, 106*, 107*, 110*, 112-113*, 115-119*)

BASIDIOLES. 42*, 91.

BIAPICULATE. More or less lemon-shaped (see limoniform). *Cortinarius pseudosalor*, *C. elatior* (Basidiospores). 111

BILATERAL GILL TRAMA (see Divergent). Boletaceae, *Paxillus involutus*, *Gomphidiaceae*, *Phylloporus* sp. (although becoming irregular with age). 61.

BILATERALLY SYMMETRICAL SPORE. 99*, 100.

BINDING HYPHAE. *Polyporus squamosus, Lentinus badius, L. crinitus, L. tigrinus.* 30.

BISCOCTIFORM. Biscuit-shaped.

BOLETIFORM. *Chroogomphus* sp., *Gomphidius* sp., Most of the North Temperate species of the Boletaceae (eg. *Suillus luteus, Leccinum scabrum, Boletus edulis* (Basidiospores). 111, 113*, 118*.

BOTULIFORM (=Allantoid). 111.

BRACHYBASIDIOLE. Modification of Brachycystidia. 91.

BRACHYCYSTIDIA. *Coprinus atramentarius, C. comatus, C. micaceus, Conocybe lactea, Bolbitius vitellinus, B. varicolor.* 72, 75*, 84*, 91, 92*.

BROOM CELLS. See Cellule en brosse or Cystide en brosse. *Marasmius plicatilis, Mycena rulantiformis* (Pileocystidia). 79*, 80.

BULLET-SHAPED (more or less equal to Stenospore and to Projectile-shaped). *Lepiota castanea, L. cristata, L. subalba, L. fulvella. 113*.*

BULLIFORM. Bubble shaped, Swollen. See Vesciculose.

BURSIFORM. Bag-like.

CALIBRATION OF THE MICROSCOPE. 8*.

CALLUS. Many species of *Galerina* (Basidiospores). 101.

CALYPTRATE. *Galerina calyptrospora, G. allospora, G. mamillata* (Basidiospores). 105, 107*, 117*.

CAPITATE. *Conocybe* subgenus *Conocybe* section *Conocybe, Conocybe spicula, C. brunnea; Entoloma helodes* (Cheilocystidia); *Coprinus curtus* (Pileocystidia); *Pholiota tuberculosa, Galerina mycenopsis, Tubaria conspersa* (Cystidia). 76, 78.

CAPITULATE. *Panaeolus sphinctrinus* (Caulocystidia), *Galerina sideroides, G. ampullaeocystis* (Cystidia). 78, 79*, 88*.

CAPUT. Head 76.

CARMINIOPHILOUS GRANULATION. (– Siderophilous). 22, 91, 93*.

126

CATENULEE. *Russula elephantina, Cortinarius piperatus* (Small chains on the spores as seen in Melzer's).

CAULOCYSTIDIA. 73*, 82*.

CRISTULEE. *Russula nigricans.* (Small chains on the spores as seen in Melzer's).

CATAHYMENIUM. Basidium not arranged in a single layer, *Lentinus sajor-caju.*

CAULOCYSTIDIA. *Nolanea cuneata, Leccinum versipellis, Coprinus* section *Setulosi, Conocybe tenera, Panaeolus sphinctrinus.* 72.

CELLULAR PILEIPELLIS. *Pluteus* section *Cellulodermi, Marasmius alliaceus, M. oreades, Psathyrella spadiceogrisea, Panaeolus sphinctrinus, Conocybe tenera, Coprinus* section *Setulosi.* 19*, 44, 46*, 55*, 59*, 64.

CELLULAR SUBHYMENIUM. *Amanita hongoi, Armillaria albolanaripes, A. ponderosa, A. luteovirens.* 63*.

CELLULAR MEDIOPELLIS. *Nolanea sericea, Mycena sanguinolenta.* 51*.

CELLULAR SUBPELLIS. *Nolanea sericea, Lactarius hygrophoroides, Hypholoma fasciculare, H. capnoides.* 51*, 59*.

CHEILOCATENULAE. *Agaricus sylvaticus, Paxillus* spp., *Phylloporus rhodoxanthus, Amanita muscaria.* 33*, 36, 74, 86*.

CHEILOCYSTIDIUM. 29*, 73*, 82*, 85-88*, 93*.

CHEMICAL REACTIONS (CHEMICAL REAGENTS). See Amyloid, Dextrinoid (=Pseudoamyloid), Carminophilous, Metachromatic, Cyanophilic. (For other examples see the text).
   Reactions with Alkali. (Potassium hydroxide, Ammonium hydroxide).
   Spores that become darker. *Conocybe tenera, Bolbitius vitellinus, Galerina unicolor.*
   Crystals in mountant. *Conocybe tenera.*
   Caulocystidia that turn red. (turn green with Ammonium hydroxide). *Psathyrella* sp.
   Granules in the trama that turn green or anthracite with Potassium hydroxide. *Anthracophyllum nigrita.*
   Pileipellis that turns reddish brown. *Cystoderma* sp.
   Yellow-Walled Cystidia in Ammonium Hydroxide. *Psathyrella squamosa.*

Reactions with concentrated Sulphuric Acid.
Diverticulate cells of *Coprinus patouillardii.*
Spores that decolorize. *Coprinus spp.*

Reactions with Congo Red. Red spores of *Chlorophyllum esculentum.*

Reactions with Melzer's (other than those listed under Amyloid or Dextrinoid)
Hyphae that turn grayish olive. *Omphalotus olearius.*
Hairs of the pileus turn gray. *Crinipellis piceae.*
Pegs of the spores. *Calocybe constricta.*

Reactions with Fuschin (see Fuschinophile Hyphae).

CHIASTOBASIDIUM. All agarics but not *Cantharellus.* 89.

CHRYSOCYSTIDIA. *Hypholoma fasciculare, H. sublateritium, H. capnoides, Stropharia semiglobata, Pholiota squarrosa, P. flammans.* 74, 84*.

CHRYSOVESSELS. *Pholiota astragalina.* 36.

CILIATE DERMATOCYSTIDIUM. *Lactarius fuliginosus, Russula heterophylla, R. virescens.* 50.

CITRINIFORM (=Limoniform). *Mycena integrella, Marasmius oreades, Panaeolus sphinctrinus, Cortinarius mucosus* (sublimoniform) (Basidiospores). 110*, 111.

CLAMP. *Phyllotopsis nidulans* (slender) (Hyphae of Pileipellis). 32, 34*, 42*.

CLAVATE. *Leptonia lividocyanula* (Pileocystidia). 75*, 76, 77*, 86*.

CLAVIFORM. *Nolanea cuneata* (Caulocystidia). 76.

CLEAVAGE SEPTUM. Frequently seen in the vegetative hyphae at the base of the basidiocarp. 32.

CLITOPILUS SPORES. *Clitopilus prunulus, C. hobsonii.* 105, 107*, 116*.

COMPLANATE. Flattened or Compressed; see *Coprinus plicatilis.* Most basidiospores are slightly compressed in side-view.

COMPRESSED. (see Complanate).

128

CONDUCTING TISSUE. Tissues that secrete and excrete substances. Includes laticiferous and oleiferous elements (*Lactarius and Russula* sp.), chrysovessels (*Pholiota and Stropharia* sp.), and gloeovessels (*Lentinellus cochleatus*). 30.

CONFLUENS TYPE CUTIS. *Collybia confluens, C. peronata, C. acervata.* 47.

CONNECTIVE TISSUE. Generative and other rapidly growing elements. *Amanita muscaria, A. phalloides, Amanita* spp., *Limacella illinita.* 30.

CONSTRICTED (=Strangulated). *Hygrocybe strangulatus* (Basidiospores). 80.

CONVERGENT GILL TRAMA. All species of *Volvariella* and *Pluteus.* 61, 62*.

COPRINOID HYMENIAL STRUCTURE. *Coprinus comatus, C. atramentarius, C. micaceus.* 91.

CORALLOID SUBHYMENIUM. *Amanita sublutea.* 63*, 64.

CORDATE. *Coprinus plicatilis, C. cordisporus* (Basidiospores). 111, 112*.

CORNUATE (=Barbellate). Cystidia of *Pluteus cervinus* and *P. salicinus.* 79*, 80, 85*.

CORONATE. Crowned.

COSCINOIDS. Dark colored conducting system with winding perforations or holes inside otherwise solid filaments. See Coscinocystidia. 36.

COSCINOCYSTIDIA. The end cells c a coscinoid. Not found in agarics. See *Gloeocantharellus.* 74.

COSTATE. *Boletellus ananas, Strobilomyces costatispora, Boletellus pallescens* (Basidiospores). 105, 106*.

CUCURBITIFORM (=Lageniform, Sicyoid). *Galerina autumnalis, Conocybe vexans, C. togularis* (Cystidia). 78.

CUNEATE. Wedge-Shaped. *Lepiota cuneatispora.* (Basidiospores) 111.

CUTICLE. An incorrect term; replaced by pileipellis. 43.

CUTIS. *Mycena sanquinolenta, Pulveroboletus ravenellii.* 51*, 74.

CYANOPHILIC BASIDIA. *Lyophyllum multiceps.* 91.

CYANOPHILIC BASIDIOSPORES. *Lepiota* sp., *Chamaemyces fracidus, Melanophyllum echinatum, Gyroporus cyanescens, Paxillus involutus, Hygrophoropsis aurantiaca.* 114.

CYANOPHILIC HYPHAE. *Crinipellis piceae.*

CYANOPHILOUS. 24, 91, 114.

CYLINDRIC. *Lentinus crinitus, Pleurotus ostreatus* (Basidiospores); *Leptonia trichomata* (Pileocystidia). 76, 77*, 109, 110*.

CYLINDRO-CLAVATE. *Lentinus* sp. (Hyphae in hyphal pegs); *Leccinum scabrum, Entoloma sericatum* (Pileocystidia); *Pluteus boudieri* (End cells of pileipellis); *Leccinum aurantiacum* (End cells of pileipellis). 76, 77*, 86*.

CYSTIDE EN BROSSE. Cystidia with prolongations and diverticulae; may cover acanthophysoid and dendrophysoid structures. Broom cells of *Mycena corticola, M. tenerrima, M. citrinomarginata; Marasmius* spp. 80.

CYSTIDIA. Sterile elements in the hymenium or terminal elements of the pellis. (See Cheilo-, pleuro-, caulo-, and pileocystidia). 73*, 75*, 77-79*, 82-88*.

CYSTIDIOID HYPHAE. Hyphae with only slightly differentiated end-cells. *Hygrocybe laeta* (margin of the gills). 34*, 36, 72, 74.

CYSTIDIOLES. A sterile cell. Either an undifferentiated or immature cystidium or a slightly enlarged or modified sterile basidium. Considered by some to be true cystidia which originate at the level as basidia and differ only slightly in size and/or shape from basidia and brachycystidia. *Conocybe tenera* (Cheilocystidia). 71.

CYSTODERM (=Cellular). Composed of sphaerocytes; a velar structure overlaying the pileipellis. *Cystoderma amianthina, Coprinus stercorarius.* A pileipellis composed of rounded cystidia-like elements — *Coprinus micaceus.* (See other examples under Cellular Pileipellis). 44, 46*.

CYTOPLASMIC PIGMENTS. *Inocybe geophylla, Bolbitius vitellinus, B. variicolor, B. reticulatus.* 36.

130

DACRYFORM (=Dacryoid, Lacryform). *Clitocybe infundibuliformis, C. gibba* (Basidiospores). 111, 112*.

DENDROPHYSIS. Not found in agarics. *Dendrochaetae russiceps, D. vallata.* 74, 75*.

DENDROPHYSOID LAYER, *Mycena tenerrima, M. corticola.*

DENSE STRUCTURE. *Lentinus torulosus, Crepidotus* sp. 50, 57*.

DERM. See specific examples of Derm, as in Trichoderm or Palisadoderm for example. 44, 55-56*.

DERMATOBASIDIA. *Pluerotus ostreatus* (in culture); *Conocybe intrusa, Boletus subsolitarius* (on the pileus); *Leccinum scabrum, L. aurantiacum, L. caprini* (on the stipe). 89-90.

DERMATOCYSTIDIA. On the outer surface of the basidiocarp. *Conocybe coprophila* (Pileocystidia); *Gerronema fibula* (Pileo- and Caulocystidia); *Panaeolus sphinctrinus* (Caulocystidia). 50, 72.

DEXTRINOID (=Pseudoamyloid). *Paxillus panuoides, Lepiota cristata, Macrolepiota procera, Leucoagaricus naucinus, Hygrophoropsis aurantiaca, Chaetocalathrous craterellus.* (Basidiospores). *Geopetalum carbonarium* (Cystidia). *Mycena* sp. (Hyphae). 25, 114.

DICHOPHYSIS. Wide angled, colored, branched (often antler-like) with terminal branchlets. Not found in Agarics. *Variaria* sp. 74, 75*.

DICHOPHYSOID STRUCTURE. *Resupinatus applicatus, R. dealbatus.* 50.

DIFFERENCE. Spore length minus spore width. 102.

DIGITATE. *Mycena epipterygia* (Cheilocystidia); *Mycena leptocephala* (cheilocystidia); *Agrocybe arvalis* (Pleurocystidia). 79*, 80.

DIMITIC. Of two kinds of hyphae, generative with binding hyphae, as in *Lentinus crinitus* and *L. tigrinus*, or with skeletal hyphae. 28.

DIMORPHIC BASIDIA. *Hygrophorus firmus, Coprinus comatus, C. atramentarius.* 89-90.

DISTAL. The apex of the basidiospore; Away from the sterigmata; Where the germ pore is located; Opposite to the Apiculus. 96, 98*

DISARTICULATING HYPHAE. *Leccinum versipellis, L. insigne, Cystoderma amianthinum, Phaeolepiota aurea, Pulveroboletus ravenelii.* 33*, 40*.

DIVERGENT GILL TRAMA. *Amanita muscaria, Catathelasma ventricosa, C. imperialis, Hygrophorus bakerensis* (fresh). 61, 62*, 68*.

DIVERTICULATE HYPHAE. *Xeromphalina fulvipes, Mycena epipterygia, M. epipterygioides* (Cheilocystidia); *Mycena tenerrima, M. corticola, Coprinus narcoticus, C. stercorarius* (Velar elements). 50, 79*, 80, 85*.

DORSAL. Adaxial side of spore. Side inner most to the axis of the basidium. 96.

DORSIVENTRAL. 96.

DRYOPHILA TYPE CUTIS. *Collybia dryophila, C. fuscopurpurea.* 47.

ECHINATE. *Mycena borealis* (Pleurocystidia); *Strobilomyces echinatus, Clavaria echinospora, Crepidotus echinospora, Inocybe calospora, Laccaria bicolor* (Basidiospores). 79*, 80, 105, 106*.

ECHINULATE. *Ripartitella squammosidisca, Gymnopilus echinulisporus, Conocybe subverrucispora, Ripartites tricholoma, Crepidotus cesati, C. variabilis* (Basidiospores). 105.

ECHINIDIA. Often applied to the shortened Broom Cell; *Mycena tenerrima.*

ELLIPSOID. Three dimensional figure giving an elliptic, optical section. 109.

ELLIPTIC. *Clitocybe* sp., *Mycena haematopus, Omphalina ericetorum, Amanita muscaria, Cortinarius lividoochraceus, Omphalotus olivascens* (Basidiospores). 109, 110*. 117-118*.

ELONGATE. A spore shape. 76.

ENCRUSTED. (see Incrusted also). *Inocybe fastigiata, I. geophylla, Mycena aurantiidisca, Gomphidius subroseus* (Pleurocystidia only), *Melanoleuca melaleuca, Hohenbuehelia petaloides.* (Cystidia). 31*, 33*, 88*.

ENDOCYSTIDIA. Chrysocystidia embedded in the hymenophoral trama found in species of *Pholiota, Stropharia,* and *Hypholoma.* 72.

ENDOSPORIUM. 101, 102*.

END VIEW OF SPORE. 116*.

ENTEROCUTIS. A cutis composed of swollen cells. *Clitocybe hydrogramma, Hygrophorus foetens.* 49*, 52*, 57*, 59*, 74.

EPIMEMBRANARY PIGMENTS (=Incrusting [encrusting] and intercellular pigments). *Boletus chrysenteron, B. porosporus, Flammulaster* sp. 37.

EPISPORIUM. 101, 102*.

EPITHELIUM (=Polycystoderm). *Cystoderma amianthinum, C. granulosa, Melanophyllum eyrei, Leccinum albellum, L. carpini, L. crocipodium, Naucoria escharoides.* 44, 46*, 55*.

EQUILATERAL. 109.

EXOSPORIUM. 101, 102*.

FABIFORM. Broad Bean Shaped. *Inocybe fastigiata* (Basidiospores)

FACE VIEW OF SPORES. 96, 117*.

FALCATE. Sickle Shaped.

FALCIFORM. Scythe-Shaped.

FALSELY VERRUCULOSE. *Calocybe constricta, C. leucocephalum* (Basidiospores).

FALSELY ECHINULATE (=Ganodermoid). *Ganoderma* sp., *Fayodia bisphaerigera.* (Basidiospores). 103, 106*, 116*.

FALSELY RUGULOSE. *Kuhneromyces mutabilis.* (Basidiospores).

FALSE SETA. (=Setiform Lamprocystidia; Setoid Cystidia).

FILIFORM CYSTIDIA. (See Cystidioid Hyphae). 74, 77*.

FOVEATE. *Boletellus betula, Porphyrellus cookei, P. subflavidus* (Basidiospores).

FUNDAMENTAL TISSUE. Inflated, multiseptate, thick-walled (more or less sclerified) hyphae of the basidiocarp. Skeletal hyphae (eg. in *Lentinus lepideus*) and fusiform skeletals sometimes included. Found in any part of a young basidiocarp in agarics. 30

FUSCHINOPHILE HYPHAE. Hyphae that react with Fuschin. *Russula* sp.

FURCATE. *Hygrophoropsis aurantiaca, Paxillus involutus, Russula* sp. (Cystidia). 80.

FUSIFORM. *Pleurotus ostreatus, Catathelasma imperialis, Inocybe lacera, Leptiota mutaespora.* (Basidiospores). 109, 110*.

FUSOID. Somewhat fusiform.

FUSOID-VENTRICOSE. *Leptonia pseudobulbipes* (Cheilocystidia). 88*.

GANODERMATOID (=Ganodermoid, Falsely Echinulate). 103.

GELATINIZED HYPHAE. *Hohenbuehelia nigra, H. petaloides, H. geogenuis, Resupinatus applicatus, R. rhacodium.* 35, 40*, 65*, 70*.

GELATINIZED SUBHYMENIUM. 69*.

GENERATIVE HYPHAE. Thin-walled, septate, undifferentiated or sometimes slightly thickened hyphae with continuous protoplast which stains intensely with cotton blue. 28, 29*.

GERM PORE (= Apical germ pore). *Bolbitius vitellinus, Conocybe tenera, Stropharia semiglobata, Panaeolus sphinctrinus.* (Basidiospores). 101.

GILL TRAMA. The hymenophoral trama of gilled basidiocarps. 60, 69*.

GLOBOSE (=Spherical). *Amanita citrina, Laccaria laccata, Russula foetens, Oudemansiella radicata, O. mucida, Limacella delicata, Mycena corticola.* (Basidiospores; actually they are all subglobose). 109, 110*.

GLOEOCYSTIDIA. *Lentinellus cochleatus, Favolaschia saccharina, Lactocollybia* sp. Uncommon in agarics. 72, 74.

GLOEOVESSELS. Those hyphae, only aseptate, connected to and possessing similar chemical characters as gloeocystidia. 36.

GRANIFORM Shaped like grains of corn. *Conocybe intrusa* (Basidiospores); Hilar plage area of certain collections of *Coprinus micaceus.*

134

GUTTULATE. *Lepista saeva, Calocybe granulosa, Tricholoma saponaceum, Clitocybe nebularis, C. clavipes, Hygrocybe conicus, H. puniceus, H. hypothejus.* (Basidiospores). 101, 118*.

HAIR-LIKE HYPHAL STRAND. *Crinipellis piceae, Chaetocalathrous craterellus.* 50, 52*, 58*.

HAIR (=Pilocystidium, not pileocystidium). *Conocybe pubescens, C. pseudopilosella.* 50.

HETEROBASIDIUM. A basidium showing septation; not found in agarics. 89.

HETERODIAMETRIC. 100.

HETEROMEROUS. Trama of the Russulaceae. 35.

HETEROMORPHUS. The cystidia on the gill face different than those on the gill margin. *Agrocybe arvalis.* 72.

HETEROTROPHIC. 89, 93*, 98, 99*.

HEXAGONAL. *Conocybe antipus, Coprinus hexagononsporus.* (Basidiospores). 114, 115*.

HILAR APPENDIX (=Hilar appendage, Apiculus). *Amanita muscaria, Crepidotus variabilis,* any rhodophylliod genus such as *Leptonia, Entoloma.* (Basidiospores). 96, 98*, 117*, 118*.

HILAR SPOT. (=Plage, Suprahilar depression). A small depression found near the hilar appendix. Amyloid in many *Russula* sp.; non-amyloid and poorly colored in *Melanoleuca* sp.; ornamented in some collections of *Coprinus micaceus;* rough in rough spores of *Galerina laevis;* smooth in the roughened spores of *Galerina hypnorum.* 98.

HILUM. The actual spore surface that makes contact with the sterigmata. 96.

HOLOBASIDIUM. A single celled basidium; typical of most agarics. 89, 92*, 93*, 97*.

HOMIOMEROUS. Composed of a single kind of hyphae strand; applied to the hymenophoral trama and typical of most agarics except the Russulaceae. 35.

HOMOMORPHUS. A gill in which the hymenium lining the face is the same as that lining the margin. *Agaricus campestris; A. hortensis.* 72.

HYMENIDERM. A cortical layer composed of hymenium-like units. *Leccinum scabrum, Boletus edulis, Suillus luteus* (Stipitipellis.) 47.

HYMENIFORM LAYER. Resembling a hymeniderm. *Simocybe centunculus, Agrocybe erebia, Strobilurus occidentalis, Conocybe laricina, C. tenera.* 46*, 47, 55*.

HYMENIAL CYSTIDIA. Cystidia found in the hynemium. See Cheilocystidia and Pleurocystidia. 72.

HYMENIUM. The surface composed of basidia and allied cells forming a reproductive layer. 60, 92*, 93*.

HYMENOPHORAL TRAMA. *Resupinatus* (gelatinized); *Conocybe tenera, Bolbitius vitellinus* (composed of inflated cells); *Hygrophorus conicus* (composed of short cells). 60, 62*, 63*, 68-70*.

HYMENOPHORE. Literally means to bear the hymenium; often applied incorrectly to the entire basidiocarp. 60.

HYMENOPODIUM. *Xeromphalina* sp., *Marasmius* sp., *Panus* sp., *Pleurotus* sp. (thick walled). *Gomphidius glutinosus, Paxillus involutus, Chroogomphus rutilus* (interwoven); *Conocybe tenera, C. lactea, C. intrusa* (regular); *Mycena galericulata* (composed of parallel, thin hyphae), *Pholiota decorata* (gelatinized). 63, 65*, 69*.

HYPHAE. Septate filamentous units of the basidiocarp in agarics. 28-38, 39-41*.

HYPHAL PEG. (Not to be confused with Buller's genetic terminology). *Lentinus crinitus* (in the hymenium). 29*, 91.

HYPHIDIA (=Hyphoids). Filiform or monilioid hyphal extensions in the hymenium of *Aleurodiscus* (=pseudophyses or dicaryoparaphysis); not found in agarics. 72, 74.

HYPHOIDS. See Hyphidia.

INAEQUIHYMENIIFEROUS. *Coprinus comatus, C. atramentarius.* (Hymenium). 90, 92*.

INAMYLOID. *Tricholoma virgatum, T. saponaceum, Clitocybe nebularis, C. clavipes, C. suaveolens, C. langei, Collybia dryophila, C. confluens, C. peronata.* (Basidiospores). 25, 114.

INCRUSTED (see Encrusted). 37, 39*, 70.

INEQUILATERAL. 96, 109, 117*.

INFLATED RAMOSE SUBHYMENIUM. *Amanita polypyramidis.* 63*, 64.

INTERCELLULAR INCRUSTATIONS. 37.

INTERCELLULAR PIGMENTS. *Cortinarius sanguineus, Chroogomphus tomentosus, Suillus granulatus, Paxillus atrotomentosus.* 37.

IRREGULARLY INCRUSTED (ENCRUSTED) HYPHAE. *Suillus brevipes, S. luteus.* 37.

INTERMIXED. (=Interwoven) HYMENOPHORAL TRAMA. *Lentinus conchatus, Hygrocybe pratensis.* 61, 62*, 69*.

INTERWOVEN. See Intermixed.

INTERRUPTED RETICULATE ORNAMENTATION in Melzer's. *Lactarius quietus, L. rufus, L. vietus.* (Basidiospore).

INTRACELLULAR INCRUSTATIONS. *Leptonia euchroa* (Pileipellis); *Leccinum insigne* (Pileipellis). 37.

INTRAPARIETAL PIGMENTS (=Membranary). 37.

INVERSE GILL TRAMA (=Convergent). *Pluteus cervinus, P. salicinus, Volvariella esculenta, V. speciosa.* 63.

IRREGULAR GILL TRAMA. 61.

ISODIAMETRIC. 61, 100.

IXOCUTIS. *Entoloma prunuloides* (possibly an ixotrichodermium), *Hygrocybe conica, Hygrophorus hypothejus,* (very difficult to tell from an ixotrichodermium). 47.

IXOENTEROCUTIS. *Rhodotus palmatus.* 47.

IXOEPITHELIUM. *Leccinum albellum* (when gelatinized).

IXOPALISADODERM. *Conocybe coprophila, Bolbitius vitellinus, B. reticulatus.* 47.

IXOHYMENIDERM. 47.

IXOMIXTOCUTIS. 47.

IXOPALISADODERM. *Conocybe coprophila, Bolbitius vitellinus, B. reticulatus.* 47.

IXOPARALLELOCUTIS. 47.

IXOTRICHODERMIUM. *Entoloma madidum, Suillus luteus, S. grevellei, Boletus badius, Leccinum olivaceoglutinosum.* 47, 58*.

LACHRYFORM. See Lacryform. 111.

LACRYFORM (=Dacryform; Lachryform) 111.

LACRYMOID. 111.

LACTIFERS. *Lactarius volemus, L. piperatus, L. vellereus.* 36.

LACUNOSE. *Porphyrellus cookei, P. subflavidus; Boletellus betula.* (Basidiospores). 105, 107*.

LAGENIFORM (=*Curcurbitiform, Sicyoid*). *Conocybe arrhenii.* 78, 87*, 88*.

LAMPROCYSTIDIUM. *Psathyrella squamosa, Inocybe dulcamara, I. geophylla, I. fastigiata.* 72, 83*.

LANCEOLATE CYSTIDIA. *Mycena corticaticeps.* 78, 79*.

LATICIFERS (=Laticiferous Hyphae). *Lactocollybia lacrimosa, Betrandia* sp., *Lactarius* sp. 36.

LATERAL STRATUM. *Amanita muscaria.* Reduced in the hymenophoral trama of *Conocybe* sp. 61, 68*.

LECYTHIFORM. *Conocybe pubescens, C. tenera, C. subovalis, C. lactea.* (Cheilocystidia). 78, 79*, 87*.

LEIOSPORE. Smooth spored.

LENTIFORM. *Psilocybe atrorufa, Concybe intrusa, Coprinus niveus, C. megalospermus, C. friesii* (Basidiospores). 109.

LEPTOCYSTIDIA. *Leptonia jubata, L. fuligineomarginata, L. serrulata.* 72, 79*, 86*, 87*, 88*.

LIGATIVE HYPHAE (=Binding Hyphae). 30.

LIMONIFORM (= Citriniform). 111.

LOBULATE. Having small lobes. *Inocybe grammata* (broad lobes), *I. oblectabilis*. (small).

LUNATE. Crescent-shaped.

MACROCYSTIDIA. 74, 75*.

MEDALLION CLAMP. *Leptonia cyanea*. 34*, 35.

MEDIOPELLIS. The middle layer in a pileipellis of three layers. 44.

MEDIOSTRATUM. *Paxillus involutus* (gelatinized); *Amanita muscaria*. 61, 65*, 68*, 70*.

MELZER'S REAGENT. 67.

MEMBRANAL PIGMENTS. *Panaeolus sphinctrinus, Concybe tenera, C. rikeniana*. 37.

MESOSPORIUM. 101, 102*.

METACHROMATIC HYPHAE. *Mycena* sp., *Agrocybe* sp. (Trama). 38.

METACHROMATIC BASIDIA. *Tricholoma* sp. 91.

METACHROMATIC METULOIDS. *Campanella* sp. 80.

METACHROMATIC SPORES. *Russula* (only the ornamentation), *Macrolepiota procera, Gerronema* sp., *Leucoagaricus* sp., *Leucocoprinus* sp. 114.

METACHROMATISM. 24, 114.

METULOIDS. *Gomphidius glutinosus, Chroogomphus tomentosus, Pluteus cervinus, Inocybe decipiens, I. fastigiata* (Inamyloid and colorless); *Copelandia* sp. (Inamyloid and colored); *Campanella* sp., (Metachromatic); *Geopetalum carbonaria* (Dextrinoid or pseudoamyloid); *Gloiocephala anastomosans* (Amyloid). 74, 75*, 79*, 83*.

MITIC SYSTEM. The analysis of the context of the basidiocarp. 28.

MIXTOCUTIS. *Nolanea staurospora, Collybia dryophila*. 47, 49*, 59*.

MONILIFORM. *Leptonia subeuchroa* (Hyphae of the pileiopellis); *Pholiota oedipus* (Cheilocystidia). 58*, 79*, 80.

MONOMITIC. *Lentinula edodes, Pleurotus ostreatus;* all fleshy agarics. 28.

MONOSTRATOUS. *Schizophyllum commune, Tubaria pellucida, T. furfuracea* (Basidiospores). 101, 117*.

MUCRO. Crested as in the cystidia of *Pluteus cervinus* and *Pleuroflammula* sp. 76.

MUCRONATE. *Leccinum scabrum* (Cheilo- and Dermatocystidia); *Copelandia cyanescens, Mycena haematopus* (Cheilocystidia); *Macrocystidia cucumis* (Cheilo- and Pleurocystidia). 78, 79*, 80.

MURICATE. With hard excrescence. *Inocybe geophylla, I. fastigiata, Melanoleuca melaleuca.* (Cystidia).

MYCOSCLERIDS. *Russula* sp. 74.

NACREOUS. Having a pearly lustre. Any gelatinized tissue as seen in alkali solutions, e.g. ixotrichodermium.

NAPIFORM. *Leptonia fulva* (some Pileocystidia). 76.

NAVICULATE. *Mycena paucilamellata, M. filiformis, M. lactea, Marasmiellus ramealis, Marasmius rotula* (Basidiospores). 111, 112*.

NECROPIGMENT. *Callistosporium colorea.* 37.

NODOSE-VERRUCOSE. *Horakia flavofusca.* (Basidiospores).

NODULOSE. *Conocybe nodulosospora, Inocybe grammata, I. petiginosa* (Basidiospores). 104*, 105, 114, 115*, 119*.

NODULOSE-PORE. 105.

NODOSE. *Inocybe asterspora, I. napipes* (Basidiospores).

OBCLAVATE. *Mycena sanguinolenta* (Cheilocystidia). 75*, 76, 78, 79*.

OBLONG. *Tubaria furfuracea* (Basidiospores). 109, 110*.

OBLONG-ELLIPTIC. *Mycena epipterygia, Geopetalum carbonaria, Schizophyllum commune* (Basidiospores). 109.

OBTUSE. *Bolbitius vitellinus* (Caulocystidia); *Xerulina chrysopepla* (Pleurocystidia); *Chamaemyces fracidus* (Pileipellis and Cystidia). 76.

OLEIFEROUS HYPHAE. *Russula emetica, Amanita vaginata.* 36, 40*, 41*.

OLEOCYSTIDIA. With oily contents. *Russula* sp.

OPEN-PORE. 96.

ORTHORHOMBIC (=Prismatic). 99*, 114.

ORTHROTROPHIC SPORE ATTACHMENT. *Hiatulopsis, Bovista, Lycoperdon, Phallus, Rhizopogon.* Not found in the agarics (in the strictest sense). 89, 99*, 100.

OVATE. *Panaeolus sphinctrinus* (Basidiospores in face view). 111, 112*, 116*, 117*.

OVAL. *Tubaria conspersa, Cortinarius crystallinus, Simocybe centunculus.* (Basidiospores). 111.

OVOID. *Conocybe intrusa* (Basidiospores).

PALISADODERM (= Palisoderm). *Leptonia serrulata* (Pileal disc), *Lepiota cristata, Bolbitius vitellinus, Conocybe farinacea.* 47, 48*, 49*, 56*.

PALISODERM. See Palisadoderm.

PARALLEL HYMENOPHORAL TRAMA. *Psathyrella velutina, Hygrophorus coccineus.* 61, 63*, 69*.

PARALLELOCUTIS. *Collybia confluens, Coprinus radiatus, C. cinereus.* 47, 57*.

PARAPHYSIS. (in agarics, = pavement cells or brachycystidia).

PAVEMENT CELLS. (See Brachycystidia).

PEDICELLATE. Not in agarics; *Bovista* (Basidiospores).

PELLICLE. *Bolbitius vetellinus, B. aleuriatus.* 43.

PELLIS (= Skin). See Pileipellis or Stipitipellis.

PERFORATE-PUNCTATE. *Boletellus betula.* (Basidiospores).

PERISPORIUM. *Coprinus narcoticus, C. stercorarius, C. sclerotiger, C. tuberosus* (Basidiospores). 101, 102*.

PHAEOCYSTIDIA. *Fayodia deusta.* 74.

PHASEOLIFORM. *Inocybe pudica, I. jurana, I. fastigiata, Phyllotopsis nidulans, Conocybe brunnea, C. septentrionalis, Coprinus domesticus,* (Basidiospores). 111, 113*.

PHYSALOMITIC. *Geopetalum carbonarium.* 30.

PIGMENT BALLS. Red brown globules within hyphae or forming free in the medium when placed in Melzer's reagent. *Leccinum quercinum.*

PILEIPELLIS. The layers constituting the outer surface of the pileus. Of a single layer in *Crepidotus* sp., *Lentinus conchatus;* two layers in Conocybe tenera, *Bolbitius vitellinus;* three layers in *Armillaria mellea.* 43, 45*, 46*, 48*, 49*, 51*, 52*, 55-59*, 73*.

PILEOCYSTIDIA (does not equal Pilocystidia). *Conocybe laricina, C. coprophila, Macrocystidia cucumis, Flammulina velutipes, Coprinus* species in the section *Setulosi.* 39*, 40*, 42*, 55-59*, 72, 73*, 82*, 86*, 88*.

PILOCYSTIDIA. (= Hair).

PILEUS TRAMA. 39*, 40*, 66.

PILOSE AGGLUTINATION. (= Hair-like Hyphal Strand).

PIP-SHAPED. *Russula ventricosipes, Mycenoporella lutea, Marasmius rotula, M. scordonius, M. oreades, M. foetidus,* species of *Collybia.* 111, 113*.

PISIFORM. Pea shaped.

PITTED-RETICULATE. *Porphyrellus subflavidus, P. cookei, Boletellus betula* (Basidiospores).

PLAGE. *Galerina vittaeformis, G. marginata, Melanoleuca melaleuca, Gymnopilus penetrans, Hebeloma crustuliniforme* (Basidiospores). 98.

PLEUROCYSTIDIA. *Psathyrella velutina, Gomphidius subroseus, Hohenbuehelia petaloides, Coprinus atramentarius, Melanoleuca melaleuca, Galerina vittaeformis.* 42, 73*, 82*.

PLURISTRATOUS CELLULAR SUPRAPELLIS (= Epithelium, Polycystoderm). 44.

POLYCYSTODERM. (=Cystoderm; Pluristratous cellular suprapellis). 44, 46*.

POLYGONAL. *Inocybe rennyi* (Basidiospores). 114, 115*, 119*.

PRISMATIC (= Orthorhombic). *Nolanea staurospora, N. xylophila.* (Basidiospores). 114, 115*, 119*.

PROFILE. 96, 117*.

PROJECTILE-SHAPED (= bullet shaped, stenospore).

PROXIMAL. End of spore attached nearest to the basidium. 96, 98*.

PRUNIFORM. *Cortinarius turbinatus.* (Basidiospores). 111.

PSEUDOAMYLOID. (= Dextrinoid).

PSEUDOCLAMPS. *Phyllotopsis nidulans* (?). 34*, 35.

PSEUDOCYSTIDIA. Extensions of conducting system, eg. gloeocystidia, chrysocystidia, phaeocystidia and macrocystidia.

PSEUDOPARARENCHYMA(-TOUS). The tissue of a primordial agaric where no differentiation has taken place.

PSEUDOPHYSIS(-ES). (= Pavement cells or Brachycystidia in agarics). 91.

PSEUDOSEPTUM. *Pseudocraterellus sinusous.* 32.

PTERATE (= ALATE). *Leucopaxillus albissimus, Cortinarius violaceus, Boletellus betula, Cortinarius punctatus* (pimpled), *C. delibutus.* (Basidiospores). 105.

PUNCTATE. 104*, 118*.

PYRIFORM (= Sublimoniform). *Cortinarius pseudosalor, Panaeolus rickenii.* (Basidiospores). 76, 77*, 78, 111, 112*.

QUADRATE. *Marasmius nigripes* (Basidiospores). 114, 115*, 119*.

QUOTIENT. 102.

RADIALLY SYMMETRICAL SPORES. 99*, 100.

RAMEALES STRUCTURE. *Marasmius rameales, Marasmiellus juniperinus.* 50, 51*, 52*, 57*.

143

RAMOSE SUBHYMENIUM. *Lepista nuda, Clitocybe nebularis, Collybia peronata.* 64.

REGULAR HYMENOPHORAL TRAMA. 61.

RENIFORM. *Inocybe fastigiata.* (Basidiospores). 111.

RETICULATE. *Lactarius chrysorrheus, L. fuliginosus, Russula fellea, R. ochroleuca, Heimiella retispora, Strobilomyces floccopus.* [*Basidiospores*]. 105, 107*.

RHODOCYBE SPORES. *Rhodocybe caelata, R. Mundula.* 105, 107*.

RHOMBOID. *Nolanea rhombispora, Flammulaster rhombispora.* (Basidiospores). 114, 115*, 119*.

RIBBED SPORES (= Subalate). *Clitopilus prunulus, Boletellus russellii.* 105, 106*.

RIND. Outer surface of the stipe; approximately equal to the stipitipellis. 43.

RING-LIKE INCRUSTATIONS. *Boletus chrysenteron, B. porosporus, Gymnopilus junonius, Flammulaster* species. 31*.

ROD-LIKE PROTRUSIONS. *Mycena filopes, M. iodiolens, M. galericulata.* 31*, 40*.

ROSTRULATE. *Mycena lactea, Marasmius juniperinus, Flammulina velutipes* (Basidiospores). 111.

ROSTRATE (= Rostellate). *Phaeocollybia* sp., *Poromycena decipiens.* (Basidiospores). 111, 113*.

ROSTRATE-VENTRICOSE. *Leptonia perfusca* (Cheilo- and Pleurocystidia).

ROSTRUM. Apex of a restrate cystidium. 76.

RUGOSE. *Psathyrella rigidipes, Panaeolina foeniscecii, Galerina vittaeformis, Rhodocybe caelata.* (Basidiospores). 103.

RUGULOSE. *Hygrophorus schulzeri* (in Melzer's), *Galerina clavata, G. mycenoides.* (Basidiospores). 103.

SARCOMITIC. *Trogia* sp. (Sarcodimitic), *Mycenella bryophila* and *M. margaritospora.* 30.

SCLEROBASIDIUM. *Armillaria mellea* complex, *A. polymyces, Aeruginospora hiemalis*. 91.

SECTIONING TECHNIQUES. 9*.

SEPTUM. A cross wall in the hyphae of the basidiocarp of agarics. 32.

SETA. Not in agarics. *Hymenochaetae* sp., *Phellinus* sp. 72, 75*.

SETIDIFORM. See Setiform. 72.

SETIFORM LAMPROCYSTIDIA. *Hohenbuehelia niger, H. petaloides*. 72, 83*.

SETOID. *Coprinus auricomus, Psathyrella conopilea* (Pileipellis).

SETULE. Brown colored unit that is more or less skillet shaped. Not in the agarics.

SICYOID (= Lageniform, Cucurbitiform).

SIDEROPHILOUS (= Carminophilous). *Lyophyllum decastes, Tephrocybe palustris, T. carbonaria, T. rancida, T. ambusta, Calocybe gambosa*. 22.

SIDE VIEW OF SPORES. 96, 116*.

SIGMOID. *Clavaria* sp. (Basidiospores). Not found in agarics. 111, 113*.

SILATE. (= Psilate). Almost smooth.

SKELETAL HYPHAE. *Geopetalum petaloides, Lentinus tigrinus, L. lepideus, Trogia* sp., *Mycenella bryophila*. 28, 29*.

SKIN. (= Cuticle, Pileipellis). 43.

SPHAEROCYST. *Russula mairei, R. emetica, R. lepida, R. vesca, R. cyanoxantha, Lactarius turpis, L. vellereus*. 33*, 35, 41*.

SPHAEROCYTE. *Amanita aspera, Coprinus sclerotiger, C. tuberosus* (Veil); *Cystoderma* (all species), *Cystogomphus* (Pileipellis). 33*, 35, 41*.

SPHAEROPEDUNCULATE. *Agrocybe erebia, Pluteus boudieri, P. nanus, P. lutescens* (Pileocystidia). 76, 86*.

SPHERICAL (= Globose). 109.

145

SPINOSE (= Echinate). 104*, 105.

SPINULOSE. 105.

SPIRAL INCRUSTATIONS. 31*.

SPORE. General term usually applied to BASIDIOSPORE.

SPOROPORE (= Germ Pore).

STELLATE. *Inocybe insignis, Pterspora, Crucispora naucorioides* (Basidiospores). 104*, 105, 114, 115*.

STENOSPORE (= Projectile shaped, bullet shaped).

STERIGMA (STERIGMATA). 89, 98*.

STICHOBASIDIUM. Not in Agarics. *Cantharellus cibarius, Craterellus cornucopioides, Clavulina* sp., *Hydnum repandum.* 90.

STIPE CROSS SECTION. *Russula* sp., *Xeromphalina cauticinalis, Coprinus.* 70*.

STIPITIPELLIS. The outer tissue of the basidiocarp stipe. 43, 48* 51*, 52*, 73*.

STRANGULATED (= Constricted). *Hygrophorus strangulatus, H. reai* (Basidiospores), *Leptonia jubata, Alboleponia sericella* (Cystidia). 79*, 80, 88*.

STRIAE. 105.

STRIATE. *Boletus chrysenteroides, Melanophyllum echinatum, Naucoria escharioides, Boletellus intermedius.* (Basidiospores). 105, 106*, 116*.

SUBALATE (= Ribbed). 105.

SUBFUSIFORM (= Boletiform).

SUBGLOBOSE. *Hygrophorus ovinus, Amanita phalloides, Clitocybula lacerata, Paragyrodon sphaerosporus.* 109, 110*.

SUBHETEROMORPHUS. *Leccinum versipellis, Suillus luteus, Strobilurus stephanocystis, Macrocystidia cucumis, Melanoleuca melaleuca.* 72.

SUBHYMENIUM. *Hygrocybe laeta* (gelatinized). *Lactarius fuliginosus.* 61, 63*, 65*, 69*.

SUBLIMONIFORM. Almost lemon shaped.

SUBOVATE. 117*.

SUBPARALLEL. 63*.

SUBPARALLEL HYMENOPHORAL TRAMA. *Naucoria* sp., *Tricholoma equestre, Hygrophorus conicus.* 61.

SUBPELLIS. The lowermost region of the pileipellis. 44.

SUBREGULAR. 61.

SUBSPHERICAL. *Amanita phalloides.* (Basidiospores). 109.

SUBULATE. *Mycena atkinsoniana* (Cheilocystidia). 78, 79*.

SUBVENTRICOSE. Almost ventricose. 76.

SUPRAHILAR DISC. (= Plage, Suprahilar Plage). 98.

SUPRAHILAR PLAGE. (= Plage, Suprahilar Disc). 114.

SUPRAPELLIS. The outermost layer of the pileipellis. 44.

SYMMETRICAL SPORES. 100.

THREE SPORED BASIDIUM. *Coprinus trisporus, Boletus edulis* subsp. *trisporus.*

TIBIIFORM. 78, 79*, 87*, 88*.

TORULOSE (= Moniliform). 80.

TORTUOSE. *Mycena tortuosa, M. Lactea.* (cells of the pileipellis; cheilocystidia).

TRAMA (= Flesh; context).

TRAMAL CYSTIDIA (= Endocystidia). 72.

TRICHIFORM (= Aculeate).

TRICHODERM (TRICHODERMIUM). *Boletus chrysenteron, Phylloporus rhodoxanthus, Entoloma fibrillosum, Paxillus atrotomentosus, Flammulaster carpophila.* 47, 48*, 56*.

TRICHODERMIAL PALISADE. *Neopaxillus echinosporus, Boletus Pruinatus, B. truncatus.* 47, 48*, 56*.

TRIMITIC. 28.

TRUNCATE. *Boletus truncatus, Stropharia ambigua, Conocybe lactea, Bolbitius vitellinus, Coprinus angulatus.* (Basidiospores). 101, 114, 117*, 118*.

TUBERCULATE. *Mycena magaritospora* (Basidiospores). 105, 116*.

TUBERCULATE-RETICULATE. 116*.

TUBERCULATE-STRIATE. *Ramaria botrytis* group, *Gomphus rettisporus, Lacrymaria velutina.* (Basidiospores). 105.

TUBE TRAMA. Hymenophoral trama between the adjacent hymenia on the face of the tubes. 60.

TURBINATE. Top shaped. 76, 77*.

TWO SPORED BASIDIUM. *Coprinus sassii, C. bisporus, Nolanea cetrata, Agaricus hortensis.* 89-90.

UNDIFFERENTIATED PELLIS. *Collybia ansema.* 44.

UTRICULATE. *Coprinus stercorarius* group. *C. tuberosus, C. narcoticus. C. sclerotiger.* 105, 107*.

UTRIFORM. *Conocybe utriformis,* (Cheilocystidia); *P. hydrophila, P. subnuda, P. vernalis* (Pleurocystidia). 78.

VACUOLAR PIGMENT. *Amanita muscaria, Leccinum versipellis, L. aurantiacum, Agaricus augustus,* (Pileocystidia); *Leptonia serrulata, Mycena haematopus, M. sanguinolenta* (Cheilocystidia). 36.

VEIL. 33*, 41*, 54*.

VENTRAL. (= Adaxial Face). 98.

VENTRICOSE. *Leccinum scabrum, Macrocystidia cucumis* (Caulocystidia); *Psilocybe subaeruginosa, P. cyanescens, Tricholompsis rutilans* (Cheilocystidia). 76, 77*.

148

VENTRICOSE-ROSTRATE. *Pholiota astragalina* (Pleurocystidia. 75*, 78, 87*, 88*, 93*.

VERRUCOSE (= warty). *Lacrymaria velutina, Leucopaxillus paradoxus, Cortinarius mucosus, Horakia flavofusca, Rhodocybe caelata, Coprinus insignis, Lyophyllum constrictum, Cortinarius raphanoides, Russula schiffneri, Rhodotus palmatus, Panaeolina foenisecii.* 103, 104*.

VERRUCULOSE. *Lentinellus cochleatus, Clitocybe flaccida, Tubaria autochthona, Ripartites tricholoma, Lepista nuda.* (Basidiospores). 103.

VERSIFORM. *Conocybe lactea* (Basidiospores); *Bolbitius vitellinus* (Cheilocystidia). 80.

VESICULATE (-OSE). *Agaricus langei, A. variegata, Termitomyces striatus, Leptonia fulva* (Pileocystidia); *Bolbitius vitellinus, B. variicolor* (Cheilocystidia). 76, 77*.

WARTY (= verrucose). 103.

WRINKLED. *Armillaria mellea* (faint), *Galerina mycenopsis.* (Basidiospores). 103.